Holding the Silences

Publisher's note—about the author

Penelope Eckersley was administrator of the Association for
Promoting Retreats when I first met her in London in 1970.
She contributed articles regularly to *The Vision* (now *Retreats*), also
to *Frontier*, *One in Christ*, *Community*, *Theoria to Theory*, and to the
Church Literature Association and St Clare Leaflets.
Somewhat surprisingly, this is her first book. Her writing began with a
journalism diploma from King's College London and a pre-war stint as
junior reporter on the *Kent & Sussex Courier*—from the South Downs
to the Himalayas, one could say. The half-century's deepening
in between included five children born during the war and austerity,
and a mature return (as a new grandmother) to King's College in the
1960s. Many will know her as a retreat conductor and spiritual
director, particularly among the Franciscan and Julian movements
and at the Dunamis organization she helped found at St James,
Piccadilly. She still lives in London, in a leafy oasis near Paddington.
She has a growing number of grandchildren and great-grandchildren.

Holding the Silences

A Nepal notebook

Penelope Eckersley

with photographs by the author

Abbey Press
Glastonbury

First published in 1998 by
Abbey Press Glastonbury
32 Norbins Road, Glastonbury, Somerset, England, BA6 9JG
email: *jim.nagel @ UKonline.co.uk*

Edited and typeset in 11-point Monotype Garamond
using *Impression Publisher* on Acorn workstations

Printed and bound in Great Britain:
colour and cover by Micro Laser Designs, Bath;
text and paper-binding by WBC Book Manufacturers, Bridgend;
limited-edition binding, by hand, by Ann Muir Marbling, Frome

A catalogue record for this book is available from the British Library

ISBN 0-9533203-0-8 sewn paper binding
ISBN 0-9533203-1-6 cloth binding

I dedicate this book in gratitude to

Anila Nawang Samten

Front cover:
• *The view from the gompa*

Back cover:
• *Khumbila, "the god of the Khumbu", with attendant clouds*

The photograph of the author on the back cover is by Roger Smeeth

Contents

Foreword

"Jump into experience while you are alive"—Kabir's saying could be one of the chapter headings of *Holding the Silences*. The Indian mystic's words describe exactly the tone and substance of Penelope Eckersley's visit to Nepal to Lawudo, a tiny Tibetan Buddhist monastery twelve thousand feet up in the Himalayas. There, at the age of 70, Penelope experienced four weeks of a Tibetan Buddhist retreat. In the epilogue she writes how she "longed to find the common ground, the shared experience" between Tibetan Buddhism and herself, an Anglican with a breadth of experience and vision, which has taken her well beyond the Church of England.

"But somehow," she writes, "we never met at the spiritual level, only at the practical." Yet that is the strength and beauty of *Holding the Silences*—coping with the cold, the food, the never-ending battle with fleas, she conveys in a most telling and closely observed way the flavour of Tibetan Buddhism.

In her reflection on her meditations Penelope compares naturally and easily parts of the Christian tradition which resonate with her experience of the people and of the harsh beauty of the Himalayas. Meister Eckhart, the Celtic tradition, Bardsey Island, St Cuthbert and Holy Island and St Francis of Assisi all find their place. *Holding the Silences* is a reminder of the limitations of all religions and points us to that which is divine in every human being and in all creation. Again and again, Penelope shows us how daily life is the best spiritual teacher.

Penelope was welcomed with humour, kindness and grace. She describes how she was accepted as part of that small monastic community. Of one thing I am certain: they will never forget the visit of this remarkable, generous woman.

Donald Reeves

rector
St James's Church, Piccadilly, London

June 1998

Preface

In 1990 I set out for Nepal to meet my English Tibetan-Buddhist friend Alison in Kathmandu and to go north with her to spend a month at a small monastery in the Solu Khumbu. I was in my seventieth year and therefore anxious to take advantage of Alison's invitation before it became physically impossible for me to make the journey. This invitation had arisen from a period when Alison and I were living in the same house. In our separate rooms and in our different ways— Buddhist and Christian—we would both spend a time of meditation each day. She was working long hours in a responsible job. I was often away from my base guiding groups or individuals in retreat and when at home spending much time in pastoral counselling, as well as with my family. The high and peaceful places of the Himalayas beckoned me.

I went intellectually ill-equipped for the experience, but I considered the chance of a direct encounter more important than spending precious time on a lot of preparatory reading. Though I was aware how our imagination and sympathy in the West are blinkered by our colonial past when faced with other faiths and cultures, I was optimistic that I could keep a fairly open mind. The reader will have to be the judge. For this is the journal of what, for me, were four inter-related encounters: the first with the majesty of the Himalayas, the second with Tibetan Buddhism, the third with the Sherpa culture of the Solu Khumbu and the last with myself, isolated from my usual social and cultural props.

During the last twenty years, while working at a demanding and interesting job, I have been involved in a four-generation family support network—firstly of my four sisters and our widowed mother as she succumbed to Alzheimer's, secondly of my daughter surviving the trauma of bankruptcy with five children of wide age range and then with her and her three brothers supporting my husband, Tim, as he faced cancer. My job involved me in encouraging many people to explore silence as essential for self-knowledge, creative awareness and spiritual growth, in guiding groups and individuals in retreat and in personal counselling. I often neglected to keep enough silent space for myself. My Tibetan-Buddhist friend Alison had spent six weeks in this small retreat centre in the Solu Khumbu and in 1989, while living with me in London, she suggested we should return there together. This book is about our journey and the times of silence I enjoyed there.

It is also the journal of four inter-related encounters: the first with the majesty of the Himalayas, the second with Tibetan Buddhism, the third with the Sherpa culture of the Solu Khumbu and the last with myself, isolated as I was from my usual social and cultural props. The first and third were the most positive—full of the excitement and the discoveries of awe-inspiring beauty and human simplicity and courage. The negativity to Tibetan Buddhism which developed in me during some periods of my stay, in spite of my warm-hearted Sherpa hosts, turned into a disappointment with myself. I longed to find the common ground with them, the common spiritual experience. In my previous encounters with other faiths this common experience had always been in meditation and silent prayer together. In such open inner country few signposts or directions are needed. Words and definitions obstruct the way. Thrown back on myself, with no shared experience of meditation when I encountered the new or unexpected in Tibetan Buddhism, I seemed driven back to words and definitions which related to my own cultural and religious background for explanation. This was a disappointment to me, as I tried to keep an open mind but longed for books and others' words to point a way. This struggle with myself was perhaps the loneliest part of my journey.

In spite of the sense of privilege as well as thankfulness with which I have returned, I realize that the common experience of the greatest value is our shared humanity and that all spiritual paths which lead us beyond ourselves also affirm the divine within each one of us. For me everyday life remains the most vital spiritual practice.

Chapter 1

My cell in the gompa

From my Nepal notebook, 20 May 1990

I am in a small and remote Tibetan Buddhist monastery, 12,000 feet up in the Himalayas. It is not as challenging an experience as I expected it to be from some points of view, but it is certainly challenging at the personal and cultural level to be sharing the extreme poverty and dirt, kindness and humour, of a Sherpa home with the monk and nuns who live here. Today I start my retreat—four weeks of silence from "carnal conversation" as the Buddhists term it—which is a new challenge, in this place which is so strange to me. This first retreat day I am taking as an orientation day. I hope that part of each day's programme will be to write in this notebook.

The Lawudo monastery I am in is at the centre of a flat terrace cut out of the mountainside. It is a three-storeyed partly wood-framed building made with stone and clay, approached by two short flights of steps. It faces south towards the Kwangde range high above the valley of the Bhute Kosi river, in the Solo Khumbu region of Nepal. Above the snow line behind it is the sharp peak of Kapsale, which is 5,583 metres high. The temple (*gompa*) occupies the whole of the first floor of this building with a canopied porch above the entrance. On the next floor are sleeping rooms for visitors and *dharma* students—I occupy one of these —also a room for processing and drying incense. All these rooms are reached by steps at the back of the building. Finally there is a large attic for storage under the roof of corrugated iron, which is reached by a wooden ladder outside the door of my room. On the eastern side of the terrace, with its tall brightly-topped pole for the prayer flag, are the living and sleeping area for the Lama's family, with the stable for the yak and dzos underneath and a wooden balcony above, off the south and west sides of the main room. Leading off the entrance area to this room is the kitchen, built against the mountainside, with no chimney and roofed with pieces of corrugated iron, beaten tin and matting kept in place by stones.

Steeply up behind these buildings to the north is the cave in which the previous Lawudo Lama lived. It now forms a shrine only lived in by the present lama when he is here. The cave is faced with a white-painted stone wall and has a small window giving onto a courtyard with some other attractive small stone buildings around it. This courtyard is reached through a high wooden door, by a low stone house, where the present lama's family lived some years ago, but which now serves only as a store. This little complex of simple stone buildings with brightly painted doors and windows has an atmosphere of calm and seclusion so that it does not surprise me that my friend Alison has installed herself in part of one of them, normally used for storing potatoes. In consequence a lot of cleaning and reorganizing has been going on. Some distance below all the other buildings are three primitive cells in a row, under the mountainside: one occupied at the moment by an American monk in retreat, one unusable and one occupied by me until yesterday night, when the rain brought the debris from the roof onto my bed and I retreated— in both meanings of the word—to the *gompa*.

The people who live in this beautiful place include Lama Thubten Zopa's mother and sister. He is the present Lawudo Lama, a *rinpoche*, a reincarnation of the old lama who lived in the cave with the courtyard. He is usually away in Dharmsala or lecturing in the West. His mother is held in great esteem. She is herself a nun and is simply called Amala— the Mother. His sister, also a nun, is called Anila—the nun. She is the hard-working centre of the place and the provider and carer for all. I look forward to knowing her better. She has helping her, and sharing her bed, a young girl called Thubten Drolkar whom she appears to have rescued from a drunken father and despairing mother with many children living in Thami, a village further up the valley below. Drolkar looks after the dzos, milks and feeds them and calls them in from the mountainside. She also helps in the kitchen and the garden. She is about fourteen and has never been to school. Representing his order of monks and in charge of the *gompa* is the only man, Thubten Norbu. He is the open-faced friendly Sherpa who embarrasses me by moving from his seat of authority on the bench next to the fire in the kitchen so that I may take a place there. He takes the yak up the mountain to collect wood and on Saturdays to Namche bazaar to fetch provisions. He makes the incense, looks after the *gompa* and manages the place.

I have begun my retreat

In the kitchen, which I miss tonight, I probably pick up my present companions—fleas, which always come to me and to which I am rather allergic. They also appreciate that welcoming, warm place, where Anila sits on her yak skin on the mud-stained wooden floor before the baked-clay open fire, feeding it with dried yak dung and bits of juniper, while she stirs the big pot over the cooking hole. Some smoke finds its way through the gap between the roof and the mountain; the rest fills the room. The wooden bench against the wall between the fireside and the door is covered with old sacks filled with wood shavings and there is a little stool for use as a table, which Anila pulls up before me as she offers me my bowl of Sherpa stew. The surroundings may be primitive to Western eyes, but everything is done with great courtesy. Food is offered in both hands with a slight inclination of the head. No one snatches anything or asks for more before being offered it, and everyone waits for all to be served before starting to eat. Opposite the bench are wooden shelves with archaic tins for flour and other foodstuffs, also cooking pots and odd-looking wooden graters whose use I have yet to discover. Hanging from nails on these shelves are a bladder of hardened sheep fat, some compacted Tibetan tea and herbs of various kinds. On the fourth side of the room is a small window and beside it, with direct access to the mountainside, a drainage hole lined with tin. Round this, on the floor, are a few tins and plastic bowls used for the preparation of food and washing of dishes, all of which is done squatting on the ground. Everything is black, either from dirt or from smoke. It is just like being transported back in time to medieval Europe.

Anila, in her blackened nun's robes of dark red and yellow and her shaved head under its red woollen cap, fits this period perfectly. So does the stew she is cooking in the big black pot as she chops the onion tops on the greasy chopping board, grates some dried turnip on the wooden grater and taking the hard sheep fat from the hook on the wall grates that too into the pot, in which chunks of potato, which is the staple diet of the Sherpa, are already cooking. The whole concoction is flavoured with dried chillies pounded in her wooden mortar, with cloves of garlic and with herbs. She has been preparing food and caring for everyone who comes to this place for nearly twenty-six years, but still, as she scoops the stew from the pot into an odd assortment of bowls, she laughs and jokes with Norbu and Drolkar about the day's events and talks to Alison and me in her excellent pidgin English. We sit in the light of the fire and the single taper stuck into a small exhausted gas cylinder. Before going across the yard and up the steps to bed I have my thermos filled with hot water for the night, as at this altitude it is important to drink plenty. I also light my candle because my torch needs a new bulb.

That is how it has been for the last few days but tonight I missed out on the warm cheerful meal round the fire. I hope I have also missed out on the fleas. At about 5:30, when it began to get dark, I went down to the kitchen for the Westerner's extra perk of getting my hot-water bottle filled from the large pan at the side of the fire and to have a mug of sweet yak-milk tea. Anila filled the hot-water bottle to bursting point so I was able to use some of the water for a warm wash in my soup-sized bowl before it got quite dark. I do not want to be waited on more than is necessary during this retreat time, so I shall walk the half mile to the standpipe in the mountainside and back for my own water. I have put the hot-water bottle to warm up my sleeping-bag, put on my nightclothes and extra jersey—for it is now cold and wet at night—and with my small candle stuck on a piece of grey stone flecked with shining mica, I have been reading as I wait for Alison to bring my supper. She is my retreat attendant, which is a recognized role in Buddhism. Reading, with the feeble flame balanced on my lap, surrounded by the immense silence and the dark, I was quite alarmed by a sudden loud, reverberating noise. It was like a deep throbbing engine of some kind, but there are no engines for many miles around, so it must be human or animal in origin. No dzo or yak could keep up such a deep sustained roar. Then I realized it must be Norbu, the monk, who sleeps below me in the *gompa*, playing a droning type of Tibetan horn. It is so strange to be sitting on my hard bed in my small wooden cell, while spread around me in the darkness beyond are all the unknown valleys with their leaping rivers, and the enormous snow-covered mountains rising to the highest peak on earth. To be here guarding this diminutive flickering pool of light, surrounded by such an eerie throbbing drone—which is itself suspended in the vast silence of this immense landscape—powerfully conveys to me the fragility of the human spirit.

But how far away I was from my Lawudo experience when I boarded the Royal Nepal Airlines plane to come here. It was then, sixteen days ago, that I began the notes in this book.

Chapter 2

Journey to the gompa

Ten minutes late taking off from Gatwick on an amazingly hot clear day, with wonderful visibility, we flew east over the Medway estuary then on over Sheppey, a small plane below us like a bright fly. Even from this height the fields of rapeseed are almost dazzling in the sun amid the patchwork of greens and browns. Over the Kent coast and out to sea, the red-brown outline of the Dogger Bank is quite clear at this height of about 9,000 feet. The ships are like silver minnows with their foaming wakes. To Frankfurt, then on to Dubai to refuel. I hope few Germans come on board because the 757 is pretty empty and I have seats one to three to myself, which bodes well for tonight.

After sandwiches and beer, as we gain height over Germany, the mosaic of fields has become smaller. The forests predominate, cut up by the straight autobahns and the great snaking rivers, but as we come down into Frankfurt, again vivid splashes of yellow rape stand out in the ordered pattern of the countryside. Hi-tech Frankfurt airport in all its polished affluence was over in an hour and we are now above the snow-patterned Alps, shining on their western slopes with a rosy light, which is in stark contrast to the eastern slopes where dark night has already taken over. From time to time a great cumulus cloud floats between us catching the pink glow and casting great grey shadows on the mountains. From up here they are not at all formidable. I wonder how this new encounter from a plane with the formidable Himalayas is going to be. I remember the amazing sight of them from the plane at early dawn on the flight home from Melbourne via Bangkok. I have an anxious passing thought of how much more formidable they are going to seem when I start to climb them.

We have just had one of those depressing refuelling stops at Dubai: ushered off the plane at 11:45 GMT after four hours of darkness but no sleep. Arab officialdom at its most intrusive—well, how do I know? but it feels like that—fat ladies in green uniforms and headscarves go through everyone's belongings. In the waiting room there were a large group of beautiful Ethiopian women about to depart for Abu Dhabi and Addis Ababa. They all had six or seven enormous duty-free bags loaded with electrical and plastic goods, from children's tricycles to video recorders and TV sets. Wives of government officials, I thought, with visas to travel and money to spend. They were all elegantly dressed and confident of themselves. Such a contrast to the pathetic starving Ethiopians and Tigréans, with the same fine profiles, we see so often on our TV screens. I could tell that many of the tourists and trekkers on our plane thoroughly disapproved of such high-profile purchasing power. We have taken some Arabs on board now and have had the third change of crew. You can tell whether they are Sherpas or Hindus by their clothes and distinctive faces. The Sherpa stewardesses wear dark-coloured *chuva*s and small striped aprons, have the high cheekbones and polished bronze skin of the people of the high altitudes; the Hindu women in their bright saris have the longer paler faces of the plains. I wonder if it is because of language that the crews are not mixed.

I have been presented with the new day's edition of *The Gulf News*; so breakfast soon, I suppose, and *no* sleep. As we taxi off, palm trees alternate with bright street lamps, while the planes of the world in their colourful profusion, each with a logo indicative of advanced technology sported on their sides, are cleaned, refuelled and re-victualled in the shimmering heat. By local time it must be about 6:30am.

After a delicious breakfast, during which I watched the dawn come up like an angry red dragon from the east, I fell asleep in the most frightfully uncomfortable position athwart my seat and the next empty one, the arms of which are fixed! We are now flying through low cloud over dusty red countryside, with scattered villages of houses of the same colour. I have no idea whether this is Pakistan or India. It is very flat, some irrigation canals but not a sign of green anywhere. Before I went to sleep we had been high above a rutted camel-coloured desert, swirled and ridged by wind, without any sign of habitation but every now and then a large white X, presumably of concrete, on the ground. Were these landing strips? Was this rugged land Afghanistan? It was the same colour as the Pamirs when we flew over them in the opposite direction, after my incredible views of the high peaks of the Himalayas in the early dawn in 1988. On that Australian plane I was given plenty of information by the crew. On this plane they think my questions odd, or perhaps even sinister. It never occurs to me that anyone should think my motives anything but a straightforward curiosity.

This is just one of the cultural and personal assumptions I carry around in my mental baggage. I suppose I want, on this journey, to be so aware and open that I am like a wax tablet with no inbuilt blemishes to distort or spoil the impression of all that is recorded on it. An impossible and unnatural ambition but I do not want too many of these prejudices and assumptions to get in the way—particularly not to get in the way of my understanding or my sharing, with Alison and her Buddhist friends. It ought to be so easy just to relax and enjoy all these new experiences moment by moment, but the judgemental thoughts slip in and take you by surprise. It is going to be a real challenge to develop my capacity for just looking, tasting, smelling and listening and to be able to recall these feelings and sensations, without mental intrusions and reservations.

Now it is about an hour later and the clouds are beginning to clear as we cross the grey-green flood valley of the Ganges in a northeasterly direction. Suddenly, way above the valley and seemingly almost on a level with the plane, are the great pink jagged peaks of the Himalayas catching the morning sun on the high snow slopes which rise above the clouds.

Chapter 3

Kopan monastery

Planes and airports may be much the same all over the world, but the smell of an airport which you have not been to before tells you something about the country. I remember my first arrival, over twenty years ago, at the then small airport of Malaga, in the early hours of the morning. There were few people about and a light dew was keeping the air still. As I stepped out of the plane onto the runway there was an overpowering smell, which I have always associated with the place: the heavy lingering sweetness of oleander, mixed with the immediacy of human urine. Kathmandu also had its smell, which it may share with other airports of the Indian subcontinent. This morning, beneath the smell of concrete dust caused by some building works and the smell of cheap petrol from the revving of many ancient taxi engines, was a pervasive mixture of spices, garlic and dung, brought with great clarity to the nostrils by the fine clear air.

Alison was there to meet me with a warm hug and we piled into one of the ancient taxis for the journey to Kopan monastery. This taxi journey was a good introduction to the difficulties of travel in the East. The springs were non-existent and as we veered off the mud roads to negotiate broken bridges or tracks which had been made impassable by the passage of an endless stream of people, animals and bicycle wheels, we were lurched from side to side and propelled against the seats in front. But I was hardly conscious of my own condition because I was so concerned for the people we were constantly spraying with mud and water. I soon learnt that our driver's disregard for the melée through which we drove was an accepted part of being in a car. Though I grew to recognize this attitude as part of the assumption that access to Western technology gave you a right to disregard the rest of humanity, I never ceased to wonder at the way in which men, women, cows and dogs, old people and even tiny children managed to avoid being crushed by the many types of vehicles which drove through them on all sides of the roads.

My well-appointed visitor's cell here leads off a balcony overlooking the nuns' quarters which are at a lower level. The whole *gompa* complex is on a small round hill overlooking the plain of Kathmandu with the great *stupa* of Bodhinath in the centre foreground. The sounds are sounds of peace, against a constant background of birdsong—so many different calls which I do not know. To listen carefully I have to get behind the chatter of the mynah birds. The *gompa* children chatter too as they play together in small groups. They laugh and sing softly as they feed the dogs and goats or help the monks and nuns as they look after the *gompa*, the buildings and the land. At this stage I feel it is so like Christian monastic life must have been in the Middle Ages, though there appears to be more friendly sharing of tasks among the sexes. These Buddhist children have been sent here, or secretly smuggled out, from Tibet, to be educated by the monks and nuns.

After a meal of vegetable soup, curried lentils and chapattis I am ready to sleep, but this is taking a long time to achieve because the whole valley, as soon as it got dark, has been filled with the restless barking of innumerable dogs, some it seems in packs, some tethered by the farms. As soon as one lot is quiet another one finds something to make its throat hoarse over. I lie back and let it all pour over me. Tomorrow is another day; this one has been a long one.

9:45pm, Monday 7 May

I have just been up to the top of the Kopan hill among the prayer flags and the fireflies and looked down on the great plain of Kathmandu surrounded by its dark ring of mountains. This plain was once a vast lake fed by the snows of the highest Himalayan peaks. The sky was clear, the moon almost full and I was surprised at how few stars I could see. The nuns had held their evening *puja* in their garden and I could still hear their gentle chanting, while in the valley some remnants of a wedding party with drums and singing were wending their way home through the fields. I sat for a long time under the tattered flags which moved in the cooler night air and reflected on how important it is for us to feel ourselves not as Buddhists, Christians, Hindus or anything else, but as human beings, connected by the one earth which sustains us, attempting to live and die with as much understanding of reality as we can bear. As I walked back down the hill I could see the light of the lanterns in all the little huts and houses inhabited by hermits, monks and visitors perched beside each steep path which spiralled down before me. By the time I reached the flatter ground giving onto the brightly decorated gateway arch, all the lanterns had been extinguished in the *gompa*, the refectories and the library. The monks' cells were dark and quiet and the nuns below our balcony had gone back into their dormitory to sleep. As I closed the door of my room a night bird called from a nearby tree and the dogs in the valley invaded the brief silence with their competitive barks and howls.

This place is like a village. All the men and women, as well as children, dogs and cows, seem to know their business and their role in the simple pattern. All the monks and nuns, of whatever age, wear the same rust-red robes and yellow shirts. Their bright brown eyes under their shaved heads look out at you with varied expressions of curiosity, friendliness or wisdom. I had a short conversation with the head lama this morning as he sat, telling his beads, by the wall of the *gompa*. I now know that I should have asked in advance to speak with him, but he was smilingly courteous and invited me to *puja* that evening. A very easy kind of deference seems to exist between the young and the old, and the children seem in no way inhibited. The teenage nuns look after the younger ones in groups of two or three, showing them how to sweep the leaves from the paths with bundles of sticks, helping them carry the water from the standpipe. The same goes for the boys who help in the fields and the kitchens. I asked if they were committed to the religious life from now on, but was told their dedication could be either confirmed or dropped when they are older. I wonder how many will leave for the uncertainties of the modern world.

As our balcony overlooks the nuns' quarters I have quickly identified with them. Their early-morning *puja* begins at six o'clock and the chanting seems to float up through the mist hanging below us in the valley. The children then sweep all the paths and steps with their branch brushes, softly talking to each other and singing in short bursts something which sounds like *didi, didi, didi,* which is a mantra for acquiring wisdom. All the nuns seem to eat and sleep in their one large simple building of brick with stone quoins and window arches and a roof of painted corrugated iron. The monks' main dormitory is of the same construction with more elaborate stonework. These older buildings on Kopan hill have the charm of the style of the buildings of the last century when the whole estate belonged to some wealthy Nepalese family.

Alison and I go to the visitors' dining room near the main *gompa* complex for our meals, which are always fresh and good. We take a tin plate, plastic mug and a spoon, which we wash up afterwards at big sinks outside the refectory. Breakfast is at 7:30 and includes slightly sweet porridge with bits of ginger and coconut in it, chapatti with peanut butter and tea. Lunch is at 11:30—soup, rice, different kinds of mixed vegetables in a spicy sauce, poppadoms or pancakes, bananas and herb tea. Supper at 7:00 is a simpler meal of soup with pancakes, ricecakes or chapattis. I really like this kind of food. I do not suppose, though, that there will be as much variety when we get to higher altitudes. Ionized water is always available from a big barrel by the *gompa* steps. I fill my own water bottle from this every day and then add a Puritab. I shall be sad to leave here for Boudha—officially Boudhanath but conversationally clipped—in two days.

So on my bed in the small room off the balcony above the nun's garden with the path twisting down the slope to the first row of village houses below, I ask myself the question. Why am I here?

All religious search is deeply personal. From the background of a conventional, but non-rigorous, Anglican Christianity, in which I was brought up, I am convinced that all the major theistic religions are speaking about the same God: "The Lord our God, the Lord is One"— the one indivisible God of Israel, the "God our Father" of Jesus Christ and therefore the God of Christianity. Islam also speaks of this One God.

During most of my lifetime, however, to be a Jew or to be a Muslim has been seen as a racial characteristic. I remember being horrified when refugees from Nazi Germany came to my parents' house and reported that Jewish Christians were being persecuted because they were of the Jewish race. Since the 1960s this racial link as well as many cultural links have been loosened, until we are reaching a free-market situation in religious beliefs. This supply-side approach to a religious philosophy has been encouraged, not only by the various gurus like the Maharishi coming from the East but also by the development of so many different cults in America.

I want to explore Buddhism not as a would-be convert looking for a sales package, but as something still rooted in a place and a culture. Alison's invitation has given me the chance to do this. I am also glad to see in practice a philosophy which has not been developed from the concept of One God but has retained the sense of holiness and the individual's response to that awareness. For it is that sense of the holy which has started me off and kept me on the path of this intensely personal search.

Chapter 4

Boudhanath

Here I am writing on my bed in the hotel room I am sharing with Alison, which overlooks the great Golden *Stupa* of Boudhanath. This is a vast structure of brick and clay painted white with a central dome above which is a stepped golden tower. There are smaller towers above white domes on each corner of the building and at the base of each tower human eyes are painted which look to the four corners of the earth. Somewhere at the centre of this building is buried one of Gautama Buddha's bones. This is a sacred place for both Buddhists and Hindus. Tomorrow is a great festival but now I have to catch up in my notebook with my last two days at Kopan.

I spent much time there exploring and taking photographs. The atmosphere here is so different that I want to try to recapture the feelings of peace and remember the views from up there. From our balcony one morning, looking down past the dark green leaves of a tree like a cork oak to a patch of sunlight in the nuns' garden, I could see two of them laying out bright-coloured grains and pulses to dry in the sun. At a lower level beyond them, a group of monks with primitive forks and spades were weaving their way downhill to work, while further down still the people of the village moved among their small rust and ochre houses, from which the mist was beginning to clear, preparing also for work in the tiny terraced fields or on the steep slopes of the mountains. At the centre of this crescent which slopes into the plain I could see the golden domes, close to which I now write, and behind them the turreted, domed and towered buildings of the cities of Kathmandu and Bhaktapur in the middle distance.

The pattern I established at Kopan was to get up at six when the nuns began to chant; I would wash, dress and go down to their small *gompa* for an hour's meditation, which was led, for visitors in English, by a Swedish nun. She did this simply and directly, with few words, inviting us to visualize the light surrounding the Buddha and then to bring that light into our own hearts. I felt drawn peacefully into this simple meditation, not unlike many which I have led myself in prayer groups and prayer workshops in many places, using the light surrounding the Christ in the same way. At this level the barriers between the religions seem so unimportant. We are all on a quest for enlightenment. We are following a path which has to a great extent already been mapped for us by our birth, but the destination sought at the end of each path is much the same—understanding and knowledge of what lies at the source of all life whether we name it God, Wisdom, the Tao or any other name. As we use silence and quiet minds to come closer to the holy ones who have led the way, we can also use the same images to bring us greater understanding.

After breakfast one morning Alison and I walked the three miles down here to book this hotel room. It was my first close encounter with Nepalese village life. It was reminiscent of China—my nearest previous experience—but seems much more friendly and open, in spite of the extreme poverty. The majority of the children go to school. The beggar children who do not are familiar throughout the East. "Allo, allo." "Wer'a yer from?" ... "Rupee? Wan'a rupee ... Wan'a rupee" and on and on until your sweets, your small change or your patience runs out. But so many children who emerge from the tiny hovels, as well as the small farms and houses, are dressed in clean white or blue shirts and grey skirts and trousers, to go to the low buildings which form the village schools. Here in Boudhanath the children of the shopkeepers and functionaries add a striped school tie. In this heat! How deeply ingrained are the habits of the Raj.

In the evening we joined the monks in their big *gompa* for the *puja*. We sat on cushions against the wall while the younger ones finished their chanting. Some of the smallest kept nodding asleep as they sat and were moved quite gently, by older ones, to a different position and then expected to keep going. The monks are more varied and individual in their chanting, less attractive and rhythmic than the nuns. We then witnessed the equivalent of a medieval disputation, with two monks standing and arguing a philosophical point. They gesticulated, advanced towards one another and underlined their arguments by quoting various authorities. They were also not above shouting at each other. It was all taken in very good part by everyone from the abbot down, who laughed at all the jokes and ended the session by shepherding the young ones to bed. Alison sponsors one of these small boys from Tibet, whose even younger sister is also here as a nun. To demand this disciplined commitment from such young children seems inappropriate to me at one level, but when I think of the little dark sheds by the rutted dirt roads where most of the Nepali people live with their hens and dogs, this ordered, sheltered life with always enough to eat and with understanding support and medical attention, makes me realize that I am making judgements from another world. Again I am reminded of medieval Europe and the role played by the monasteries in the life and education of children.

Last night was full moon and preparations here for the Newari festival at the Boudhanath *stupa* began. The Buddhists, many of them Sherpas and Tibetans who had come down from the mountains, were dressed in their national dress, the women in dark coloured *chuva*—a long-skirted, sleeveless wrap-over garment which ties at the back—and with which they wear a bright-coloured shirt or jumper. They all have bright headscarves and their dark hair in one thick plait at the back. The married women wear a short apron of striped material. All the men wear their clothes with a certain style, some with fur-lined jackets over one shoulder, like Hungarian hussars, and often have coloured shirts and red braids in their hair. They circumambulate the *stupa* in a clockwise direction often in village groups or family parties. This is an important form of devotion. I talked to one good-looking young couple who had come down from the Solu Khumbu for the ceremonies. He had spent some time as a trekkers' porter, so spoke a little English. They had left their two young children with his mother and after fulfilling their religious duties they would have a day's sightseeing and shopping in Kathmandu. They walked before me in silence round the highest level of the *stupa*, meditating with a mantra as their fingers moved round their *malla*s (strings of wooden beads like a rosary).

Built into the walls of the *stupa* at ground level and at the top walking level below the golden towers are rows of large wooden prayer wheels with mantras carved on them—among others, always the dominant mantra, *Om mani padme hum*. The pilgrims spin the prayer wheels with their hands as they circumambulate at this level and at all three terraced levels of the building, monks and pilgrims prostrate themselves. Again proceeding clockwise, some of them with leather guards and wood blocks to protect their knees and hands. All these devotional activities gain merit in a future life. There is no conversation. The silence is broken only by the odd barking dog or crying child in the village below, which serves only to emphasize the gentle shuffle of feet going round and round.

As darkness fell, lights came on in the houses surrounding the square and candles were lit at all levels on the *stupa*. It was beautiful and solemn, not least because of the quietness which pervaded the place. Tomorrow the noise and confusion will begin, but tonight was serious and prayerful. After some delicious spring rolls at a little Sherpa café on the square Alison and I joined the perambulators again at the top level of the *stupa*. After several rounds I sat on a ledge and looked at all the changing patterns of light and shadow created by the thousands of little candle flames which were moved in the air with the passage of the pilgrims and the great long strings of white and yellow prayer flags all hanging from the central tower across to the other towers and pinnacles, like the spokes of a vast wheel being prayed by the wind in the moonlight. This place and these people drew prayers of thankfulness from me for the chance to share this time of dedication with them and as I turned round towards the town, where the dogs were again at their usual night-time activities of scavenging and barking, the more solid patterns of shadow cast by the moon's light fell across the roofs and walls of the houses, packed tight together, along the sides of the now nearly deserted road. Just before the ten-o'clock curfew, imposed since the recent revolution, sent everyone indoors, Alison and I walked back to our hotel through the warm air, heavy with the smells coming from the creek—which serves as an open sewer—mixed with the smoky smells of candles and incense.

Chapter 5

Newari festival and Bhaktapur

Thursday 10 May

At 4:30 this morning the brass gong at the monastery on the edge of the *stupa* square boomed out for the early *puja* of the festival. Quite soon afterwards large groups of school children moved into the square to make their perambulations. They seemed overawed and well behaved, with the little ones whispering to each other and pointing to the things which impressed them, until moved on by the teachers. There were Buddhist children from the schools which are attached to the many different lama traditions from Tibet now based in this part of Nepal and Hindu children from state and private schools. As Alison and I moved into the square through the ornate painted gateway from the main road, I could see that devotions had taken place by the large *lingam* just beyond the entrance. It was surrounded with fresh rice offerings and heavily daubed with red betel juice. I am really struck by the way Buddhists and Hindus share this ceremony and this place. Maybe I do not adequately understand what is going on, and though I appreciate Alison's reluctance to overload me with her own Western Buddhist perceptions, perhaps she does not know a lot either. Round by the entrance to the *stupa* itself, where the steps go up to the higher levels, in a little visitor's temple with another *lingam* in the adjoining courtyard outside, and small statues of Ganesh and Shiva, as well as an ancient Buddha figure, I begin to feel strongly the common forces at work here from tantra to B'on and beyond. I wonder with all the mix of ethnic groups around us whether

Nepal, as the only remaining Hindu kingdom, observes a caste system or not, and what the pressures for democracy following the recent revolution will do for these simple expressions of faith.

Today there are many more monks than yesterday, both individually perambulating or with groups of friends. Among them are Western as well as Sherpa and Tibetan faces. Their red robes have become a major element in the kaleidoscope of colours. Much more numerous also are the bright saris of the Hindu women, particularly of the wealthy ones coming to give alms to the beggars, who, from early dawn, have been sitting on the brick pavement surrounding the *stupa* building. For this is a festival of prayer and almsgiving. The Hindus are having a great *puja* round a vast mound of donated saffron rice, which is decorated with fruit and flowers like a huge sand-castle. At a higher level the Sherpas chant their prayers round a bonfire onto which they throw incense and rice as offerings for a good harvest. Among the Sherpa men are some elders with great fur hats embroidered with gold. All carry their carved *malla* beads either round their necks or wrists or in their hands. As I sit outside our café I watch the groups of beggars round the *stupa*, some with a bowl or just an outstretched hand, some with a lot of children and many poor thin girls with just one baby at the breast. There are men with amputated limbs and people of all ages with deformities of many kinds. Sitting among the beggars are also groups of moneychangers, with tower-like piles of rupees before them, willing to change the larger currency denominations of the wealthy for distribution to the poor. I wonder what commission they take. The beggars sit in a resigned and, in some cases, even cheerful mood, while the multi-coloured crowd moves past them. The Hindu women in bright saris, accompanied by their children, who for today are on holiday from school, go round with plastic bags full of coins putting a few into each outstretched hand. Some successful pleaders get more, some are completely ignored. There is an underlying fatalism about the whole scene.

I have had the particular attention of a very simple, toothless young man in rags, with a permanent smile on his face. I do not want to give him rupees because it annoys the young café proprietors. They come out and shoo him away from time to time. He goes on grinning and I raise my hands in a farewell gesture, but he is soon back. The other beggar paying me great attention is a very dark-skinned girl of about twelve with nothing on but a filthy transparent garment like a Western child's puff-sleeved party dress. She stands some way off and watches all my movements. I offer her a sweet, which she solemnly takes and sucks. When this is finished she indicates that she wants me to take her photograph. This seems an easy request and I smile at her as I take my camera, but she remains extremely serious and keeps her dark eyes under her matted hair on my face, as I record her thin body under its inadequate covering. Meanwhile the general day-to-day life of the place goes on. The traders in the small shops which line the space around the *stupa* do an especially good trade from the occasional tourist, while the purveyors of cut melon, soft drinks and fried snacks, with their bundles or little carts, do well from the pilgrims and the locals. Meanwhile the cows wander about in an unconcerned way picking up anything edible they can get their tongues round, the wealthy distribute alms and the devout turn the prayerwheels or perambulate in colourful silent groups.

Later in the day Alison and I took a taxi to Bhaktapur, which is the most Hindu of the four ancient cities of the plain and quite different in atmosphere from Boudha, dominated as it is by red-brick Hindu temples rising like pyramids to steeply-eaved roofs and reached by steep flights of stone steps with attendant statues at both sides. The main street wound up the hill between warm red-brick houses with balconies, doors and windows all of carved wood of amazing complexity. The squares of the city were paved in these same small bricks in intricate patterns, flanked by four- and five-storeyed houses reminiscent in some ways of the houses of Sienna or Cortona crossed with an English Tudor building; however, the carving of all the decorative wooden windowframes and balconies, eaves and bargeboards are complicated and sinuous in a quite Indian way. I bought a thick cotton dress with red stripes and bands of hand-blocked flowers in dark blue. It seemed to fit me quite well, which pleased the young man who had designed it and owned the shop. While I was trying it on, two rather sophisticated men in white suits were sitting at an elaborately carved window on the top floor of the house across the square, drinking coffee and taking in the scene. We went to see some of the most famous of this delicate carving in an old temple which is now a museum. Then, after a really uneatable meal of kerosene-soaked noodles, we returned to Kathmandu in a very crowded local bus. I was standing pressed against a man with a live chicken under his arm. Returning to Boudha in a motor rickshaw—the cheapest form of taxi— as we were jerking across the potholes into the main street, our way was blocked by an excited procession. There were banners and pipe-and-drum bands and the inevitable accompaniment of young boys on the periphery, shouting and rushing up and down. Eventually we realized the cause was a lumbering elephant with the town dignitaries in a decorated howdah on its back, bringing the Newari festival to a close.

Chapter 6

Preparing to go north

Today we came into Kathmandu with a great list of things to get done before setting off tomorrow. We began by picking up stuff from Lama Zopa Rinpoche's centre to take to Lawudo, then changed traveller's cheques on the "black" behind the counter of a trekking-gear shop, with a Chinese woman from, I think, Singapore, whom Alison had dealt with on a previous visit. I could not help thinking how lucky I am to have such an experienced guide. I would never have trusted myself to this whole scene, even if I had been able to get into it. In the same way her experience of the waiting and red tape at the tourist office, which we encountered when applying for our trekking permits, seemed much less frustrating than they would have felt if I had been doing it on my own.

Then Alison had business about books, lost in the post to the US, at the Pilgrim publishing house, so I went into the Bistro Café to write postcards round the world to the family—my last chance for a month or more. Alison thinks the Bistro is one of the cleanest cafés in Kathmandu. "All salads guaranteed washed in treated water." It was certainly an excellent lunch of stuffed aubergine and spiced tea, in the middle of which there was a downpour. This is a good thing once a day, as it takes the surface filth off the streets and brings a fresher smell. We went next to the market area where the number of small shops and street traders gives you the most bewildering choice. As I am not sure how long I shall be in Kathmandu on my way back I bought small presents of Tibetan caps and waistcoats for the great-grandchildren and some beads from the wide selection, which hang in a vivid confusion of colour from the roofs of the stalls and all round the windows and doors of the shops, for some of my granddaughters. Finally I found a not-too-smelly sleeping-bag to hire in Freak Street, named thus because it became the favourite street of the hippies in the 1960s and '70s. Since that time the Nepalese have made it much more expensive for Western tourists, imposing taxes at the airport and a minimum amount of hard currency to be spent every day. However, by Western standards it is still very cheap to live here. Alison had a last commission: to find, among the little shops with tin-ware, mats and plastic bowls piled up in front and inside them, a good strong paraffin lamp to take to Lawudo. It cost almost exactly what she had gained by changing money on "the black" and is badly wanted by the family up there.

I am now sitting at the first-floor window of a restaurant overlooking Durbar Square, while Alison goes off to visit a young English evangelical Christian who has been imprisoned for trying to make converts. Alison is an admirable supporter of human rights everywhere. Below me, at the corner of Freak Street, the brightly painted bicycle-rickshaws wait for hire. From the collapsible bamboo folding hoods hang streamers of different colours and above them attached to a lamp post is a sign which reads "Smooth Journey"! Not likely on these roads through these crowds, though I believe the sign points to a travel agency which would probably offer an equally rough ride! Behind the rickshaws, sitting on the patterned brick paving of the square, are traders of all kinds of metal goods, brass pots intricately decorated, candle-holders and jars of many shapes. I never look long at metal artefacts because the material has no appeal for me, whereas I will always stop to look at and feel things made of wood. One of the most pleasing things about much of the fine wood carving here on the outside of buildings is the way it has weathered and worn to a fine grey patina. This is so of the wooden elements of the old Royal Palace which forms one side of the square. Among the vendors squatting among their wares are a woman surrounded by children and crawling babies, selling cut coconut from a bowl, and another cooking dhal cakes on a charcoal fire, while a man with a barrow does a brisk trade in poppadoms. There are also traders wandering about with flutes stuck onto a branched bamboo so that they look like parts of a walking tree. As the traders press these elegant little instruments on passing tourists they will play them from time to time. This adds to the pleasant noises of the sun-filled square below me and combines with the calls of children playing on their way home from school, women splashing water from a standpipe as they wash their brass pots and a trader's cry which cuts across the general chatter of the late afternoon.

Sitting at this window above the square and listening to the enormous variety of sounds enables me to pick out by sight the source of any particular sound when I want to, focus on it for a bit, enjoy both the sight and the sound, and then let it drop back again into the general background of assorted noises. This is one of the most pleasant ways of re-focusing on the inner quiet reflection which such circumstances allow. It would be so easy to allow my senses to flit constantly back and forth between the strange and constantly moving sights and sounds, but I am happy to allow them to merge into a vivid background, by which my inner reflective silence is held—and I am curiously refreshed rather than exhausted.

Friday 18 May

It is over a week since I last wrote in this notebook. In that time I have crammed in amazing experiences which I must recall before they dim in the face of so much which is new to me. That I am here at all seems a small miracle. Often I felt I would not make it—*but*—to go back to Friday 11 May.

After a taxi ride to the airport at 5:30am to catch our plane, which was to leave at seven o'clock, we had a two-and-a-half-hour wait because visibility was poor at the airstrip at Lukla, to which we were going and from which we began our climb. By the time fourteen of us had clambered into the small twin-engined Fokker, the mist had lifted enough for cameras to be clicking and for us to see some superb views of the mountains and valleys as we moved north across them. It was a forty-five-minute flight and we could watch the pilot bring us down

through heavy cloud for a manual landing at Lukla airstrip, a steeply
rising area of roughly flat ground between some green fields and
surrounding rock. We humped our packs over a wall into the village. On
first sight it seemed a very drab place after the colours and crowds of
Kathmandu. The whole was a dominant monotone of grey stone and
mud-coloured paths. I had my first sight into a dark Sherpa home as I
ducked after Alison through the low door of a trekkers' "lodge". Alison
knew this lodge owner, who gave us some most welcome hot porridge,
and Alison started to negotiate for porters to take our packs. Even
before we had entered the house a smiling Sherpa woman with bright
cheeks was offering her services and saying she would take both packs.
But we refused, saying we would take two days to Namche (little did we
know then about the limits of my climbing ability!) and asked her to find
a companion. I only had time to finish my porridge when Mingma was
back with a young boy called Donbardo and we agreed with them for
100 rupees a day each.

   Then we set out, Alison and I carrying our smaller day packs and
the other two our heavier stuff. As we passed through the northern part
of the village, across the dirty cobbled paths, past dirty-looking women
and children who came to the front of their wooden and stone houses to
watch us, I felt embarrassed by my thoughts, by my strangeness in this
setting and by their poverty, but I did not really have time to deal with it.
The Lukla people must see so many comparatively affluent Western
trekkers setting out over this rough path that I can understand their
rather surly looks of resentment. They seemed so much less cheerful and
friendly than the other Sherpas we encountered on the way. At first our
path led downhill into the valley of the Dudh Kosi river. We were passed
by large numbers of trekkers coming from the Everest area, Lake
Gokyo, Thyanboche or just Namche bazaar. They were a very
cosmopolitan lot in every sort and condition of exhaustion or
exuberance. You could tell the professionals from the others by the state
of their gear. The baggage of the experienced was neatly stowed, easy to
handle and locate in their packs, while some people had lopsided packs
with bedrolls and clothing hanging out at all angles. Behind us our plane
companions were moving also in our direction interspersed with Sherpas
carrying the most improbable loads on their backs in cone-shaped wicker

baskets, held by a leather strap across the forehead. Apart from what is carried by the much slower yaks, all the villages and valley farms above Lukla, including Namche, rely for their needs on these men, women and boys. Some of the young boys are often barefoot or so poorly clad and shod that you cannot imagine how they endure it. They carry great coils of piping, piles of planks, metal cooking pots, panes of glass, bags of rice or cans of Coke. These motley loads kept passing us and disappearing up the valley as we descended into the riverbed and followed the steep path north. Then I began to feel how weak I was for such a climb in the unusually hot sun for May.

Alison's tall body and long legs were striding out ahead of me, and breathless and exhausted I had to ask for pauses so that I could look at things and even longer pauses for refreshment. The great range of mountains on the far side of the Dudh Kosi began to rise steeply as the valley broadened out. By our rocky track were vivid dwarf irises and dark orange-veined leaves of spurge, also tiny pale blue gentians and masses of wild strawberries. Single yellow roses were clambering over the stunted conifers and juniper, interspersed with occasional birches and alders. I made a mental record through my eyes, but could not spare the energy to get out a notebook—I was being really massively absorbed in keeping going. Eventually I began to find a rhythm of walking and breathing which would lessen the ache in my panting lungs and pounding heart. I had my husband Tim's stick with me. It had been cut by him from a knotted hazel and topped with the knobbled, weathered vertebra of a sheep found on the Raasay hills in Scotland many years ago and now well polished with use. It was a great help with my balance on stony ground and propped me up for short pauses which were not long enough to flop down on a wayside rock.

At about midday we stopped for a good break and a meal of soup, boiled potatoes and tea. I had left Tim's cotton hat in the café on Durbar Square so had to tie a scarf round my head because the sun was getting so hot. In the afternoon I plodded on and Alison was very patient with my slow progress. We often came upon Mingma and Donbardo, leaning our packs against the stone walls at the side of the track to allow us to catch up. Mingma was touchingly concerned for me and halfway through the afternoon insisted on taking my small pack as an addition to her load.

I felt pathetically feeble as I gave it to her, after transferring my water bottle to Alison's load. Mingma and Donbardo on their own could probably have been in Namche by now, and by tonight Mingma might even have got to her home beyond. As it was, we took three days to Namche! But time seems no problem in these mountains and as they were being paid they also enjoyed it.

Chapter 7

Phakding to Josale

In the late afternoon we stopped at a trekking lodge at the small village of Phakding called Apple Pie Lodge. Apple pie was on offer in many lodges in the area, but Alison chose this one as she had had a meal here before. The proprietor recognized her as she welcomed us and we were shown to single rooms off the main dormitory. These dormitories are large wooden extensions to the Sherpa's house filled with wooden beds. On these the trekker can put his sleeping-bag and, with luck, get a thin foam mattress. The only occupant was a young Scot from Aberdeen University researching a thesis on ritual purity in Sherpa society.

The nicest part of these night-time stops is gathering round the fire in the Sherpa kitchen. With us that evening were the village schoolmaster and eight-year-old Pemba, the son of the house, to whom he gives extra tuition. Mingma and Donbardo joined in the talk and laughter and Mingma helped with preparing the meal. I'm not sure whether porters would get a free bed in return for this help. Certainly Donbardo had brought his own food in his small cloth bag. Mingma too had all her possessions in such a bag. They never fully undress to sleep, removing only the *chuva* and apron which reveals the long woollen tights underneath. During the afternoon it had been pretty hot—my arms and face got quite sunburnt—but they wear the same clothes summer and winter, some older women tying an oval-shaped pad to the back in the cold weather to keep their kidneys warm.

Tables and benches were round the walls enclosing the stove of brick and baked clay on which the pots cook. It was good to sit back there as the candles were lit on the table, watching the animated faces as they talked, watching the dexterity and grace with which the woman moved the large pots about to prepare our meal and to smell the wood smoke and listen to the river rushing across the rocks below the small plot of maize opposite our window. At the corner of this plot was the wooden shed, suspended above the falling ground, which serves as the only kind of lavatory in these places. Water for washing came from a pipe in the hill on this side of the track. Donbardo fetched more water for cooking and washing from this source when needed and all their nut-brown faces seemed polished in the light from the fire.

In lodges on such frequented tracks you get a written menu with idiosyncratic English spelling which includes things like potato pancakes, Sherpa stew made with vegetables, peppers and garlic, *momo*s, which are small steamed dumplings filled with chopped vegetables, perhaps noodles of some kind with yak cheese and always the heavy Sherpa bread made from brown flour on a griddle. I cannot remember what we ate, perhaps a cheese omelette, but our hostess gave us excellent peach and apple wine, which began to relax my weary muscles. They certainly needed it! She was very serious as she cooked, telling Pemba to be careful as he handed us our plates, which he did with customary courtesy with both hands and a slight forward movement. Nothing is done in a hurry and you must never take or snatch, always wait to be given. They do not take a "no" easily, always pressing you with more. After our hostess had finished the important business of cooking she relaxed also and, removing her coloured scarf from her head, combed her long black hair which shone in the firelight. I had an idea that she did this for the schoolmaster.

I was bitten by some insect in the night but otherwise slept well, out of sheer exhaustion. In the morning, before washing at the pipe, I was able to find a spot on the mountainside behind the lodge, not too overlooked by the rest of the village. I manage much better on my own with nature for these morning rituals than in the putrid sheds, after long practice on family camping holidays. After a breakfast of porridge we pressed on up the valley, sometimes climbing zigzag rocky paths more like uneven staircases, sometimes descending steeply to the river level and several times crossing it on wire suspension bridges which, from a distance as we approached them, looked as if they were constructed of string. After yesterday's slow progress on my part Alison had decided that we would have to take three days getting to Namche. Mingma and Donbardo loyally agreed to stay with us. Mingma was worried because of my age and attentively kept staying behind or waiting to allow me to catch up. On this track there are many small tea-houses at which you can stop and get a drink or maybe some griddle bread. This I found much too indigestible to walk on, but the whole party having accepted my limitations I felt much less guilty about these preferences or about holding up our progress than I had before. Alison took great care of me and we paused to look at the flowers and the amazing views whenever I wanted to. But my eyes kept being dragged back from the overhanging crags covered in clematis, the enormous white boulders washed by the bounding river or the many sparkling waterfalls, to the immediate problem at my feet: a wooden plank bridge, wet with spray, to be negotiated without slipping, rocks which skidded beneath me on a steep incline or a sudden downhill stretch which left my calf muscles aching. By the middle of the day, the heat and the altitude meant I needed a good break for lunch. Porters still passed us in both directions but there were no longer many trekkers going up. It has not been a good season for them because of the political troubles in the country. The local people all seemed friendly as we exchanged our *namaste*s in passing and the smiling children in their ragged clothes called out "Allo, Allo" at the approaches to the villages. The skin of these people seems to have taken on some of the colour of the soil, which is a rich reddy-brown. Boys and girls, when small, have their hair close-cropped and both wear trousers and often no shoes. Most of them look pretty well fed, in spite of many running noses and have these bright red polished cheeks under their sultana-brown eyes.

During this day we passed through two larger villages and crossed the river twice on rocking suspension bridges. Sometimes the tops of the mountains were hidden in cloud, which often also swirled round the valley below us. There were lots of wrens and small babblers in the surrounding scrub and trees, and ravens were busy near all the villages. Suddenly, at a certain altitude, the brilliant yellow flowers of the *Wallichii* spurge—which had been beside the track in damp places since Lukla—

came out: great golden cups ringed by large shiny orange-veined leaves. We also saw violets and many different kinds of primula near the streams which rushed across our path. All the time I was gradually getting better at timing my breathing to my puffing breath and shortened footsteps, but at the back of my mind I was dreading the even steeper climb up to Namche the next day and wondered if I would ever make it. Eating the odd snack helped and during the afternoon we bought some good yak cheese from a little teahouse perched above the river. We ate this sitting on a stone wall with some biscuits from my pocket. In the late afternoon we reached Josale and stopped at the first lodge in the village, as it was owned by a friend of Mingma. The valley by now had closed round us, with great frothing waterfalls on the far side. The lodge also was darker and more primitive than the one of the previous night, but again there was a water pipe running from the mountainside so it was possible to wash off a bit of the dirt and sweat of the climb.

At this lodge we were joined by two Englishmen teaching at a government school in Kathmandu. They had walked up from Lukla that day with one porter—who was the school gardener—carrying all their stuff. They were experienced climbers who planned to go beyond Gokyo to the Everest base camp, so had all sorts of tinned goodies with them. One of them was a Nepali speaker who gave us useful bits of information. He also revealed all sorts of information about himself, being the kind of affable talker and drinker who starts by creating interest and ends by being a bore. At these lodges you write down in a scruffy notebook your evening's orders of food and drink. There was a long list of *rakshi* (the home-made Sherpa spirit) after his name. It was late by the time Mingma and her friend produced food and as the kitchen had filled up with porters and local people, some of us ate in the dormitory in which all of us, of both sexes, slept. A disturbed stomach, caused by taking Maloprin prescribed by my London doctor (an anti-malarial drug which is not necessary at this height), caught up with me in the night. However, there was a wonderful moon to light my way up the mountain slope and breathtaking views across the river to the waterfall crashing down in a silver torrent.

Chapter 8

Josale to Lawudo

Sunday 13 May

I set off this morning before the others on the path to Namche. The silver cataract on the far side of the steep valley was still in shadow but the mountains ahead were catching the sunlight above the snowline. The swinging wire bridge, crossing the ravine just below our lodge, was the longest and most perilous in its movement of all the bridges of this kind we have so far crossed. With the help of my stick I began the steep climb on the other side, concentrating on synchronizing my breathing, heartbeat and footpace. I seemed to be given a mantra to hold all this together and to carry me through a rather dreaded day—"This is the day which the Lord has made; rejoice and be glad in it." It fitted my rhythm perfectly. As the others caught up and then overtook me, I spoke little. I know that Alison understood that I was better left on my own and needed the concentration and silence. Even when breathing was difficult, just "rejoice and be glad" was enough to keep me steady and I knew I was going to be all right. I remembered the mantras we shared and prayed on the Rochester Cathedral 850th-anniversary pilgrimage. Groups of pilgrims had started from Bec in Normandy and from English places with Benedictine connections, while our group had started from the Tower of London; for this and Rochester had both been founded by Gundulf the monk from Bec. It was only when we got to Namche that I realized it was my first Sunday in the Solu Khumbu.

The day before, as we passed through the National Parks checkpoint where you have to show your passes, we encountered a small party on the way down, with a woman on a pony who was being jogged up and down as the creature negotiated the rocky ground. She shouted to us that she was on her way down because she had had altitude sickness just beyond Namche. Now that I was actually on this stretch of the path I felt quite confident that I was going to be able to keep going.

We crossed the Dudh Kosi river twice more. The first bridge, only just above the bounding white water, was constructed in the most ingenious way with planks of wood cantilevered out from between vast boulders. The second, in great contrast, was the Hillary high suspension bridge, which considerably shortens the journey compared with the old route. Then, turning east, we followed the course of the Bhute Kosi, a tributary of the Dhud Kosi which flows below us here. We were then on the final steep stretch, the melted snow flowing off the mountain between the rivers, forming little rivulets across our path. About halfway between Namche and the junction of the two rivers it is possible, on the rare occasions when the cloud does not intervene, to go a bit off the track and get a look at Everest. At this point there is a small teahouse called, predictably, Everest View. Here we stopped and got tea but no view. On this leg of our journey we encountered many people on the way down, with whom we exchanged greetings and news. In addition the strings of porters seemed to be more numerous and the yak trains had begun again as tracks from many other places converged on Namche. There were several Nepalis going to Namche on business, including the head of the construction firm who had built the Hillary bridge. He was on his way to collect money he was still owed—from whom, was not clear. All he was carrying was a battered briefcase and a black umbrella. By late morning I was feeling fairly tired, but sooner than I had expected we rounded the last shoulder of rock before Namche and there was the village in a fold of the mountains dominated by the peaks of Khumbila —the God of the Khumbu—snow-capped and glistening in the sun.

Namche is a village where the track north to Everest and the western track to Thami, as well as many other routes, converge. At the centre are steep stony crossroads which are the focus of village life. Other paths lead off in various directions and every Saturday a market is held on a flat area below the eastern slopes. The Khunde hospital, funded by the Sir Edmund Hillary Trust, is a bit further north and the village boasts a small hydro-electric company providing a limited amount of light. The large stones edging the roads at the crossing form vantage points of observation and gossip for all those moving up and down. Alison had a lodge in mind which was just north of this crossing, which was probably on the Kopan Buddhist network, but neither of us liked the small viewless room much. We knew Mingma was anxious to get back to her village. So before exploring other lodges we paid her and Donbardo off, adding a bit to our agreed price in appreciation of their patience at my slowness. It was sad to say goodbye to our faithful and cheerful pack-people, especially the caring and gentle Mingma.

After some lunch of potato pancake in a little lodge by the crossroads, we went across to Pasang Kami's. PK, as he seems to be universally called, is quite a well known, Westernized Sherpa. I had heard about him from Elizabeth Forster, who trekked solo in this area some decades ago when in her seventies. I could tell therefore that Alison thought that his place would be too Western and not right for us, but the tall building had lots of space and views south across the valley. So we moved in our heavy packs and asked for room for two nights. Only then did we explore the outdoor facilities on the ground below the lodge, where I was confronted by the filthiest loo yet encountered and with no natural cover anywhere near as an alternative for me! *But* immediately adjacent to it was a primitive shower. PK's solar panels provided a little warm water so it was possible to take a shower and wash my hair. I am now writing in the lodge, which has three floors of accommodation for guests and family with lots of windows overlooking the valley and mountains beyond. On the top floor is the traditional Sherpa kitchen, off which I have a small corner room to myself. Alison is meditating cross-legged on her bed in the dormitory, looking towards the windowsill where she has set up her shrine. Beyond the wooden partition dividing my room from the kitchen I can hear the family chatter as they clear up the meal. They fed us well in the third-floor dining room with an international assortment of trekkers, including our voluble *rakshi*-drinking English friend from the night before. In the street below lighted lamps come and go and there are sudden bursts of shouting and laughter from young boys at the corner of the steep street.

Monday 14 May

Acclimatization day in Namche. Less exertion, so less panting. Alison and I took washing down to a point where water is piped to a communal washing place and flows on as a stream to power several great prayerwheels. I took photos for my daughter, who shares my delight in communal washing places. I looked at the five or six shops which have trekking gear for sale or rent, with a surprisingly wide selection of Sherpa and Western clothes and Tibetan rugs. I replaced my hat left in Kathmandu with a green cotton job. Alison went off to visit the local *gompa* while I zigzagged slowly around the rocky paths, took photographs and watched the women and men with their babies, with whom they love to play, and the children running up and down between the houses. I also watched the young girl whom PK seems to employ to carry water in a plastic container to his lodge from the pipe where we washed our clothes this morning. All day long this child of twelve or so walks up and down carrying the water on her back. This pipe must be the only one in the whole village. The stream which feeds it runs into the stone-lined basin in which we did our washing and then falls more steeply through a stone channel on the east of the valley. As it falls it turns the big prayerwheels housed in a line of small stone buildings. By a path towards the west ridge of the valley are a row of equally big prayerwheels under a protective wooden roof. People push these prayerwheels round in passing as they did perambulating round the Boudha *stupa*. All nature helps in their prayer. The water of the stream runs like a voice over the carved mantras on the wooden wheels under the stone shelters; the wind prays the mantra as it flutters the flags on the buildings in the courtyards and where the mountain paths meet. The work-worn hands of simple people turn the sacred texts which they cannot read, but in which they share. The movements of water, wind and hands keep the prayers flowing.

• **Kopan: *Young nuns cleaning***

overleaf: • **Kopan: *Monks' puja on the hilltop***
• **Mingma with my pack crossing the Dudh Kosi above Josale**

Chapter 9

Today to Lawudo

I am thinking of my youngest son because today it is his birthday. New York seems a long way away. I hope he has a happy day. We were up pretty early, having organized with PK last night for two porters to Lawudo. He found us a deaf Sherpa who had climbed Kwangde with a German mountaineering party and a simple young boy with a smiley face. We warned them as we set off on the northwestern path that we would be slow and asked them to go ahead to Phurte—the next village—and wait for us. To start, it was a lovely gentle walk on a smooth path lined with pink-barked birches and yellow rhododendrons. The pervasive clematis montana was nearly out and there were patches of deep-mauve violets. We climbed up the side of the Bhute Kosi valley with Khumbila to the right of us and the Kwangde range towering to the left of us across the river. Phurte is a pretty little village involved with a forestry nursery, as it is urgent for Nepal to replace the trees which are constantly being cut down for firewood. In spite of the National Park status, where such cutting is forbidden, it is rare for anyone to be prosecuted in these remote mountains. How else would they cook or keep warm in the winter? But soil erosion is obvious everywhere, so hydro-electric schemes are increasingly important. We crossed a good bridge over a stream—there

• *Party at Apple Pie Lodge: lodgekeeper and Mingma in doorway,*
  Donbardo, me, Pemba and schoolmaster

is no shortage of water, but the levels vary widely with the seasons, which is a problem when building dams for power generation.

As we turned north round a high spur of the mountain it was getting hot though it was only 10am. I pushed myself a bit too much to gain the ridge and began to feel dizzier and dizzier. Alison sent the porters ahead and I kept resting in the shade of a series of small *stupa*s which had been built along the side of the path, but eventually I had to give up and crawl into the shade of a juniper bush. It is amazing what comfort you can find in the shade of a stunted tree and the uneven feel of the ground when you really need them. Alison put her pack under my knees and I agreed to be sensible and eat and drink something, though all I really wanted to do was pant and sleep. It was about eleven o'clock and coming up to the hottest time of the day. We talked about going back to Namche in case it was altitude sickness, but I decided to stay put in the shade of my bush and rest. At about twelve I got up but still felt giddy, so we decided that Alison would go on to the little village of Mende, which lay between us and Lawudo, to get help and advice. I slept.

At about two I woke up feeling much better and with no disorientation. I got up to test for giddiness and felt OK. It didn't seem so steep ahead after all, so I thought I would give it a short try. So I walked slowly, using my stick and stopping often. Again OK. Now a problem. If I went gently on I would be abandoning our rucksacks, which included both our cameras and other gear, but there were no people about and the great relief for Alison would be to see me well and upright. Also if it took only a short time up to Mende, then more quickly down to fetch them. So, on I went slowly, slowly. I noticed the juniper and arbutus beside the path and a few violets, but nothing else. After rounding a rocky promontory the path became less steep and soon the *stupa* at Mende and the stone walls surrounding the village fields came in sight. A young woman passed me and smiled warmly. She had nothing but a Sherpa's small cloth bag in her hands. So I felt I had made the right decision about our stuff. I also felt fine and quite triumphant, but I doubt if I would have managed it with our packs.

Coming to the Mende *stupa* I sat down on the stone ledge at its base and looked up at the Lawudo *gompa*, with its tall prayer pole, high above me on the rocky slope. I thought I saw someone on the terrace, so shouted.

Some people were working by one of the farm buildings. They started to gesticulate and shout back. But of course I could not understand them so I began to walk along the top of the fields towards the *gompa*, when a voice behind me shouted, "Is that Pen?" My relief and surprise tumbled over together at hearing my name called in English in this remote place. It was Alison's American Buddhist friend Merry, who spends some time in a cave up here each year. It was amazing how this apparently empty mountain came to life. Alison had been galvanizing everyone. Here was Merry with tea, Sherpa bread and, yes, marmalade, to sustain me, while Alison had taken the porters up to the *gompa* to be fed and then rushed nearly a mile across the curve of the mountainside to the cave of a blind lama for advice. I needed the tea by then, for I had foolishly not even brought up my water bottle. After about an hour resting, drinking and talking by the *stupa* I said I thought we had better get going so that Alison should know on her return from the lama that, whatever his predictions, I was actually there. Merry having retrieved our gear from the place where I had left it, we started up the steep twisting trail to Lawudo. Young Westerners—"Injies", a corruption of English, to the Sherpa—can walk very quickly at these heights (12,000 feet) and on this ground, once they have got used to it. The mountain people of course rush up and down like goats. We were soon joined by the American monk Harry, who also lives a part of the year in another cave by the blind lama that Alison was consulting. Though delighted with all this support I also began to wonder about Alison's description of the remoteness of the place.

Harry reported that the lama's advice had been a bit conflicting. At the first throw of the *mos*—a form of prediction rather like the *I Ching*—he said, "Go back to Namche," then after tea, chat and another throw, he said, "Perhaps there is a quick recovery"! Harry, having seen two figures moving slowly up the mountainside, had decided that the latter was the truth. He reassured Alison and came down to meet us. While Merry went ahead he escorted me by easy stages to the *gompa*, were there was great rejoicing, more tea-drinking, more offerings of food and, clearly, more strange experiences waiting for me. Alison and I had a good hug.

So these are the notes on my journey which led me to this high, remote monastery and my wooden cell, smelling of incense and lit by a guttering candle at the silent heart of it.

Chapter 10

A visit to the blind lama

I had for long looked forward to the silence and peace in this place.
Alison and I had talked of it after she had made a nine-week retreat here
two years ago. Some of Lama Zopa Rinpoche's *dharma* students from the
West come here for that purpose, but I as an unknown Westerner had to
leave it to Alison to make the arrangements for me. As I am not a
Buddhist, this also served as an introduction. Their acceptance seems to
me a cause of great thankfulness. It is also a cause of thankfulness and
wonder that I actually got here and that I am now embarked on a
marvellous and probably challenging time. Most *dharma* students would,
I gather, have many of their meditations and practices prescribed for
them in retreat. I travel light in many ways. My only preparation has been
to try to let go of expectations and patterns of previous experience.
Towards that end, also literally to travel light, the only spiritual books I
have with me are my small india-paper Authorized Version of the Bible
and the Penguin *Upanishads*. In my diary I made a rough estimate of how
I would spend my time each day, but already I know that has to be
abandoned, because when the cloud lifts and the sun comes out it is a
precious time to be sharing in the immensity of the world around me. I
already feel that there is not enough time to take in and be truly aware of
all this natural beauty. So high-altitude nature is going to be the major
background and focus for my meditations. I have also come here with no
expectation of this being a time of special spiritual experience.

The tradition which surrounds me is such a visual one. Again I am
reminded of the European Middle Ages: the brightly painted *gompa* with

all its statues and portraits of Buddhas and *bodhisattva*s, each now
traditionally stylized in posture and colour; the many other deities
representing principles and powers; before them, the offerings, some
already being enjoyed by the mice, as well as the flowers (real and plastic);
the coloured ribbons and white *kata*s—blessed scarves—which abound.
In some ways you could call it all a vulgar presentation of religion for
simple and largely illiterate people, but that would be patronizing as well
as a personal aesthetic judgement. It reminds me forcibly of the interior
treatment of fourteenth-century European cathedrals. The wall-
paintings and gilded statues of the saints, the judgements and dooms, the
gargoyles and misericords, were employing a colourful tradition and local
craftsmen in the same way. This emphasis on the visual is also present in
the personal shrine which each Tibetan *dharma* student, and all the
hermits here, use for a focus during meditational practice.

Because of the visual emphasis I began to regret not having
brought with me a picture of my favourite thirteenth-century Japanese
statue of Amitabha—the Buddha of Infinite Light. This is a different
Buddha aspect from that depicted below me in the *gompa* of Chenrezi,
the Tibetan Buddha of Compassion. My small picture of a peaceful
human form in meditation, one hand held out in offering and the other
raised in blessing, would be a much easier image for me to work with
than the nine-headed, sixteen-armed version below me. I find so many
cultural blocks to this in myself which I will have to give time to.
Meanwhile the only Christian symbols which I have here with me are a
small wooden hand cross carved by a Poor Clare friend and the
Franciscan Third Order cross round my neck. But I remembered that
when I chose the King James Bible for its india-paper lightness, not
because it was my usual companion, I noticed one or two simple
cards given to me over the years by different people between the pages.
So I shook the Bible and the cards came out, and they have provided me
with an unplanned visual focus for some of my times of prayer and
reflection.

There is a wooden embrasure to the window of my cell with a
rough seat in it. I sit at one corner of this seat and over my left shoulder
—if the weather is clear—look down towards the valley of the Bhute
Kosi river and the village of Thami to the southwest. Onto the panel of

the recess on the right side of the window I have pinned a bright-coloured hand-painted handkerchief given to me by my granddaughter Nancy. Above this there was a nail already in the wood. This is fortunate because nails are precious and I would not want to ask for one. They are expensive and heavy to carry up from Namche. This nail is to be the home of my Franciscan cross. Below it on the bright handkerchief, I have pinned up, with my few remaining pins, the cards which fell out of my Bible.

They are also, in their own way, cheap and simple. They are gifts from friends and acquaintances hardly remembered. I can see, however, that they have great meditative potential for this time and place—perhaps particularly for this reason. One, the origin of which I do know, is a black-and-white photograph of St Cuthbert's cross, taken on Holy Island by my husband, when he was already being treated for cancer. It is in the form of a bookmark, and beneath the photograph, written in Tim's clear calligraphic hand, a quotation from Bede about St Cuthbert: "He regarded the labour of helping the weaker brethren as the equivalent of prayer." Below this I have pinned a two-toned card of St Francis, arms and hands open to the sky and "*Pax et Bonum*" written round the edge. On the other side of the small hanging cross I have placed a roughly printed Russian card of the ikon of Our Lady of Zigorsk, and below this a card of the modern stained-glass window of Julian of Norwich from her shrine, and at the centre bottom the familiar coloured reproduction from Maria Lach of Rublev's ikon of the Trinity. I already have a small branch of the plant—I think juniper—which Norbu uses in his incense and a bunch of vivid little mountain violets in an old jar that Alison has found me, as well as a weather-worn, wind-polished grey stone. With all else that lies around me what more could I add to the spiritual potential of my small shrine and what further retreat programme do I need? However, I do need to be aware of how difficult it is going to be for me to let go of a critical and assessing attitude to this form of Buddhism, and the circumstances in which it exists here.

Yesterday I watched Anila, just in from milking the dzos because Drolkar was busy in one of the fields belonging to the *gompa*, settle down on her yak skin before the fire to peel potatoes and go through all the processes of cooking a meal. She cooks one for us and a different one for her mother, who has digestive troubles. She has no culinary aids of any kind, such as we take for granted. I could not help feeling resentful on her behalf about her brother, Lama Zopa, who is upheld by the devotion of this family and basks in the admiration of many well-off Western devotees. He maybe lives a sacrificial life as an ascetic but can fly around the world to his next teaching or conference. Then I thought of myself: one of those able to afford to come here from a city where I live in comfort, but where more than 18,000 people have no homes of their own. Forego judgement, observe, just *be*—be aware.

The day before I began my retreat Alison and I, gaining height all the time, walked round the side of the mountain, which forms the head of the valley I look onto from my cell window. It is near the head of this cwm that Merry, Harry and the blind lama with his daughter and grandchild live. We planned to visit him to thank him for his help when I had my setback on the way up. Like all the old hermit caves round here Merry's is dug out under a great rock and then faced and floored with wood. A large part of the interior was taken up by her shrine, very gilded and ornate. At an angle from her meditation bench in front of it, was her bed and another bench. Under the small window in the wooden wall were shelves for all her domestic stuff, and shelves by her bed for her books. It seemed well organized and comfortable. Alison told me that she had never seen Harry's cave, but had been told by Merry that it was more primitive. We all sat on a big rock in the sun to drink tea and were visited by a shy creature with fang-like front teeth: musk deer. We also saw a little pika, a small grey furry creature a bit larger than a hedgehog. These animals went quietly about their business, nibbling the tree-bark or the shoots of plants, but seemed quite unafraid of us if we remained still. They are more at home here than at Lawudo because the undergrowth and shrubs are more abundant, there is more water and no grazing animals.

Later we set off to go further up the mountain to visit the blind lama. He is a member of the old Tibetan sect of *naljorpa*, whose lamas are not monks but marry and have children. There have been six generations of lamas in his family in this remote place under the peak of Mount Kapsale. He had a son, who was receiving the teachings to succeed him and also two little grandsons, the eldest of which was also expected to be a lama. Much of the spiritual tradition of Tibet is handed on orally and each sect has its own major practice and *dharma*. Alison told me that as the old man realized he was going blind he wanted to hand on this knowledge to his son and grandson. So the man and the small boy were being initiated together by this venerable figure. Some way through this initiation a certain ritual had to take place which involved the son going down to the village of Thami to buy some material or something for the rite. He got extremely drunk—perhaps he also took medication or drugs of some kind—and in spite of much care from the Thami people he died. Not long afterwards the youngest grandson, who had been weak from birth, died also. Her husband's death meant that the poor mother had to return to her own family, leaving her other, now her only, son to continue the lineage and be brought up by his grandfather and his young aunt—a nun who cared for the old man.

It is quite probable that the young man, the son, was feeling increasingly trapped by the weight of the tradition he was inheriting and the expectations of his old father. Perhaps, if he had taken part in the proposed ritual, the trap would have closed for him. However simple a lifestyle these people live they are intelligent and aware of the outside world. I wonder how long these traditions can hold. What will the future be for this small boy with the cropped hair, who ran out of the dark cave in his red monk's robe to greet us? It was apparent that Harry had a good relationship with him. They say he is difficult for his aunt to control, that he loses his temper. No wonder: he is only eight years old and has lost his father, mother and brother to a tradition which binds him, but which he cannot yet understand. It also binds his young aunt to him, and the old man, in virtual domestic slavery in this extremely remote place. However, in spite of all these thoughts rushing through my mind I could not help being impressed by the peaceful, happy atmosphere and the venerable figure in white tunic and trousers, with his white hair and long beard, looking like a picture of a Chinese sage as he sat on his bed-seat crosslegged by the fire. He lifted his blind eyes as his daughter told him who had come to visit him, and Alison and I both knelt to offer him a *kata* in gratitude for his rather conflicting advice, as well as to ask his blessing. While we were there we were joined by a Sherpa man for whom the lama is a spiritual guide. His daughter gave us all tea and as we left

the little boy shouted goodbye and followed us a short distance through
the garden of vegetable beds, watered by a clear stream which babbled
over the rocks. I was not insensitive to the positive side of this beautiful
sad place, which I trust I will be able to return to.

I am still consumed by fleas and in this cold misty weather I cannot
hang clothes or sleeping-bag out in the fresh air, for they would get very
damp and there is nowhere to dry them. I did, however, get a few clothes
washed in wonderfully soft rainwater in a new plastic bucket which
Norbu bought for me in Namche market last Saturday. He allowed me to
hang this washing on a cord across the ceiling of the attic among the
stacked bedding and the smell of incense. I saw him doing some washing
today too, kneading his long russet robe in a few inches of water in a
large bowl on the kitchen floor. I have also seen two or three pairs of
socks drying on bushes, so I must modify my ideas about our Sherpa
household's cleanliness! I have also had to modify my romantic
impression of the horn sounds yesterday evening. Norbu was playing a
tape in the *gompa*! He powers his tape recorder with a small solar battery
which I have now seen being recharged in the sun. I discovered the truth
this morning when the sound began again. The paradoxes of this place
are so intriguing. While the solar-powered tape recorder is playing in the
gompa, Anila is sitting on a large stone in the courtyard to milk the dzos
and the old lady, Amala, in her corner seat-bed in the main room, which
is like the blind lama's, is turning her big prayerwheel with a satisfied
expression, probably because she has just collected a good pile of yak
turds and put them to dry in the sun on the balcony for fuel.

Chapter 11

My battle with the fleas

Tuesday 22 May

Sunshine again—what a difference. I am sitting on the rock behind the *gompa*. Behind me is my flea-infested sleeping bag getting a good airing and the clothes I washed yesterday now really drying on the trees. Norbu has put a wet robe onto the matting on the roof of the kitchen, where it will get kippered by the smoke from underneath and dried by the sun on top. Perhaps this constant smoking of everything—even clean clothes—is what inhibits them from getting badly bitten by fleas. A thin-skinned pale person like me, who is unkippered, is clearly a good bite.

Living in the folds of these great mountains is an intimidating experience, even in the sunshine. I can feel how it has influenced the development of the Sherpa mind and Tibetan religion. It is a deep spiritual influence, not unlike the influence of the dark fiords and short days on the spirit and psychology of Norsemen like Ibsen. When Buddhism came north into this area from India, bringing with it also elements of Hindu tantra, it encountered the old B'on religion of the high Himalayas. Since the beginnings of human habitation here these people must have felt the need to placate the hostile, immutable forces around them. B'on developed from a form of animism, retaining many sacrificial rituals, some elements of which were incorporated into Tibetan Buddhism. The *chod* ceremonies and practices probably stem from B'on. I see some parallels with Christianity's encounter with Druidism, which was taking place, certainly in Ireland, at about the same time. The Celtic Christians took over many of the deities—or divine aspects, as Buddhism would call them—as well as the sacred sites and ritual practices of their forebears. In the same way Tibetans inherited and have partially retained much from B'on.

Another odd parallel with Ireland is the dependence on potatoes. These must have been introduced into Ireland in the fifteenth century when explorers brought them back from America, but they were introduced into Nepal only about one hundred and fifty years ago by the British Raj. Before that many more kinds of grain were grown on any available flat place: millet, buckwheat and barley. Potatoes must have made life considerably easier for the Sherpas, as all the grain would have had to be milled or pounded by hand or carried great distances to a water mill in the valleys. Potato varieties here are of the small waxy kind— despite excellent open fires for baking the large floury ones, they are unavailable. Maybe the soil is too rocky, though apparently some King Edwards have just been introduced into Nepal and are doing well. In any case, potatoes are cultivated wherever there is a level area of earth and the patches are surrounded with freestone walls, as in Connemara.

It is odd to be reminded of these similarities when so much else in the landscape is utterly different. There is always a sense, in the open windswept landscape of western Ireland, of the nearness of the sea: the gulls behind the plough, the smells of seaweed used as fertilizer and the sense of space stretching beyond the distant horizons are like a constant awareness of it behind the eyes. What a contrast to these enclosed, often cloud-filled, valleys dominated by fold after fold of harsh, immovable mountains. I wonder if my strange feeling of similarity is because both these circumstances challenge, and at the same time isolate, the inhabitants of these places. The sea isolates the inhabitants of the western isles. The challenge of the sea has never been far from the smoke-filled stone and turf cabins of Ireland. The proximity to great height is always challenging the people of the smoke-filled wood and stone cabins of the Khumbu. The fear and awe inspired here in these small isolated communities by their environment must have been a powerful influence in the development of this form of Buddhism—one in which profound psychological awareness of the human mind and spirit have, for many hundreds of years, been part of their accepted wisdom, handed down from lama to lama in an oral tradition. This is something which again they share with the Celtic Irish. Even sitting here in the sunlight I can understand that when the outer world of winter ice and snow becomes inaccessible and the darkness is unrelieved by artificial light, the inner world must, perforce, become the primary focus.

I feel slightly irritated when I get diverted by these historical thoughts and geographical connections—they were not what I intended for these notes or as subjects for my mountain meditations. But after all, I am not giving myself an "Ignatian retreat" but allowing myself to record my stream of consciousness. However, when reading them back when I return home, how I *feel* is going to be more important and informative to me than how I think or what I am thinking about.

My tights and socks are waving like prayer flags from the trees and twice my sleeping-bag has taken off in the high wind and had to be retrieved with difficulty from down the mountainside. Meanwhile old Amala, in her russet-red cap and robe, has made her circumambulations of the *gompa*, which she does every day between eleven and midday. Leaning on an old ski stick, she climbs up and down the steps of all the different levels of the building, her wrinkled face full of composure and purpose as she half-audibly mumbles her mantra.

This afternoon I have been reading about Chenrezi, the patron deity of Tibet, the Buddha of compassion. His mantra is the powerful *Om mani padme hum*—the jewel in the heart of the lotus—the centre of stillness and silence beyond time. This mantra I first remember using in Gandalf's Garden in Chelsea in the heady early days of flower-power in the 1960s. Here it is one of the things which help me to relate to the place. But, in spite of this and other aspects of a warm sense of relatedness to these Sherpa people, I am finding it difficult to relate to the Buddhist iconography in these regions. This apparent chaos must be partly because they have sanctified and taken over the local deities from the old religion, but also because the Vedic and tantric influence means that for every manifestation or Buddha aspect depicted, the opposite energy has also to be shown. Thus Chenrezi, who here appears totally male as he aggressively wards off evil, is given a female counterpart, the peaceful green goddess Tara. It seems that as Avolokita—the Sanskrit Buddha of compassion—moved east, Tara often replaced him until, as

in China where he is called Kuan Yin, he has a female appearance. I find
all this intellectually intriguing, but devotionally disruptive. For prayer
purposes I found, in Hong Kong and China, that Chinese Buddhism,
where only a few *bodhisattva*s and the historical Buddha—Gautama
Sakyamuni—were generally displayed in the remaining temples, this
simplicity was much more helpful to me. However, I am here, with the
direct and still living and developing results of that great *naljorpa* Padma
Sambhava, who brought Buddhism to this region in the eighth century.

Quite soon we will be celebrating Nyung Na, a feast of fasting and
dedication to Chenrezi, marking the Buddha's birthday, which takes place
at the full moon of June. Alison has lent me the text of the ritual which
has been translated into English by Merry. When you read through any
ritual texts they always seem rather wordy. They are necessarily for
involvement and shared performance rather than for literary scrutiny, but
this does appear amazingly ornate. This may be due to the detailed and
explicit descriptions of the visualizations which are to be undertaken by
the devotees. They are richly evocative visual meditations which leave
little room for the imagination of the individual. The baroque language
of the English translation is full of a sense of colour; indeed it evokes all
the senses in such a way that the powerful imagery enters directly into
the psyche and must have seemed a potent key to the inner world.
Through these visualizations, light and colour could be developed and
experienced when the outer world remained dark and hard. Perhaps this
is also what now moves the young Western men and women who come
to this tradition from our grim and intimidating modern cities. This type
of meditation must have been gradually developed as a way into and
metaphor for the inner spiritual experience by the various lama lineages
and grown as part of the increasing wisdom of the tradition. In any case
I must really listen to this language of Buddhism and not find excuses to
misinterpret it.

Complete devotion to your guru is a central element of today's
commitment for all Tibetan Buddhist *dharma* students from the West.
The complex philosophy of reincarnation, as well as the idea of gaining
"merit" by devotional practices and good behaviour, needs a spiritual
guide. The goal is enlightenment—the *bodhisattva* vow—not only for
yourself but also for all sentient beings. *Bodhisattva*s are enlightened

beings who choose to remain in this life to help others. A very detailed visualization technique is used in the Nyung Na ritual, with its roots in tantric practice. Tantra aims at a transformation of human personality through mantra, ritual and worship. A guru advises practices which are suited to the particular temperament and needs of each individual. This is clearly the guru's role and I suppose my own guru is what I miss here. Perhaps it would have been better if I had stayed longer at Kopan, where I could have had some conversations with one of the older monks with a knowledge of English. I certainly miss the shared early-morning meditation and the simplicity of the Swedish nun's words that began my day there.

"My mind," I read in the Nyung Na text, "having the aspect of inseparability of the nature of myself and of the deity, transforms into a moon disk. Upon it the sound aspect of the mantra resounding in space is established, having the aspect of written letters, like pure mercury clinging to golden sand." I can feel how such pictures can feed the spirituality of these dark valleys between the high peaks, or how they can speak to people in the dark streets between the concrete buildings. Unfortunately, for me, they are like the ornate verbal equivalent of the decorations in the *gompa*. They seem too precise to leave room for my imagination, though there are a wealth of symbols and archetypes to relate to. Through Jung we know that these should stimulate the creative levels of personality. I am aware also that working with them can have a powerful influence on the life and behaviour of an individual and therefore need to be used with safeguards, which I am not sure are always present when young *dharma* students are involved with them here. The rituals often include fasting, which can make people even more suggestible. I would make a bad student because my experience in helping people who have been "religiously" manipulated has been added to my natural cynicism. However, I would think these students would not be encouraged to take part in a ceremony like Nyung Na without the permission of their lama, or, I imagine, in any tantric visualizations without an experienced teacher. Perhaps I am a bit jealous because these reservations will make it difficult for me to take part in the celebrations wholeheartedly.

But I have been thinking that this exercise in expanding

consciousness and identification with a Buddha-aspect in some ways reminds me of Eckhart. As in Eckhart, all duality is denied: "... The light rays then return ... and absorb back into one's own mind, which is in the form of moon, lotus and mantra garland ..." says the text. "Let God be God in you," wrote Eckhart in his *Tracts and Sermons*. "I do not find God outside myself nor conceive him excepting as my own and in me." At the end of this long section on identification with the deity in the Nyung Na text is a note: "At this point one meditates on the divine appearance of oneself as the deity." Here "deity" in the text and "God" in Eckhart are being used in such different ways that comparison has to end, but to get to this point with the imaginative eye, when all around you points to powerlessness, is a most affirming process. Again I thought of Eckhart: "The eye with which I see God is the eye with which he sees me."

Included in this Nyung Na text is a confession prayer which ends: "I confess all my sins ... I rejoice in all my merits." This seems a nice balance. There is also a mantra for keeping pure moral conduct. I do hope I may be able to take part in the celebrations at some point. I have a reproduction of a *thangka* of Chenrezi above my bed—with only four arms, I am glad to say! I begin to warm to him and it seems good to have it there. Tomorrow I am going to work with a very different model of compassion: Cuthbert of Lindisfarne.

Chapter 12

Solitude and community

Wednesday 23 May

At about 4:30 this morning Norbu put his horn tape on in the *gompa* at
pretty full volume. I expect that is the time he normally gets up to make
his early *puja*. I lay looking out at the gradual illumination of the peaks of
the mountain range called Tangi Ragi Tau, which dominate the distant
western skyline which I see from my window. It is a staggering outline
which was gradually revealed by the slanting pink glow of dawn, while all
the lower mountain outlines between here and Thami remained in black
night. The light was so vibrant and clear that I hoped for another sunny
day, but by six o'clock the clouds had come up from the river below and
enveloped us in cold and damp again.

The pattern of my silence since beginning my retreat is punctuated
by meals. I go down to the kitchen to fetch my breakfast and my lunch
myself, to keep in contact with the Sherpa family and to minimize their
waiting on me. Therefore I have not adopted any inflexible rules about
no conversation. I am not sure that Alison approves. I feel that my
conversations with, and greater understanding of, the family is a very
important part of my experience here. Today I allowed myself, because
of the cold, to eat my *tsampa* by the kitchen fire. Anila herself is always
trying to persuade me to do this and it is not the only adaptation I am
prepared to make because of the weather. In fact, as the weather changes
so fast, I can really make no plans and I think that is all part of the reality
of living up here. I therefore go along with what happens hour by hour.

When in cold cloud read, meditate and write; when the sun comes through get out, wander, birdwatch, take photographs and continue to meditate. Not a bad piece of learning for someone who likes to feel she has got things organized!

Writing is the only thing possible for me at the moment because Norbu is down in the *gompa* engaged in some extremely noisy devotions of his own. I wonder whether this is because it is a special day or because he has had an argument with Anila. Certainly the latter has occurred and he is not speaking to her—perhaps that is part of his devotions. However, I am finding his activities make mine impossible. Perhaps the silence I have been so looking forward to finding here is only realizable out on the mountain. I shall see as time goes on. I tried reading Psalm 18 to find a focus for concentration: "I love you, Yahweh, my strength." But I don't really like it in the Authorized Version, in spite of the majesty of the thunderings from heaven—and I am close enough here to "the thick clouds of the skies". By the time I got to the splendid language of the more warlike verses at the end I was into my "comparative-studies mode": thinking about how our Hebrew roots help us to keep our "enemies" out there, with none of the sense of interiority I get with Buddhism.

Norbu is now chanting to the accompaniment of a metal gong. The air reverberates and I am enclosed in sound as in the clouds. I think he may be chanting his mantra. Anyway it is a wonderful noise as it combines with the waves of sound from the horn and the gong or drums. It is *not* the silence of high places today. I relax and lose myself in each moment. The sound envelops and holds me and I am lost in its throbbing life.

This experience was an unexpectedly good one. It certainly moved me away from the comparative-studies mode in my head. During the small pauses in the drumbeats Norbu's chanting of *Om*—or more accurately *Aum*—came through. "*O–aum. O–aum*"—the heart of the lotus, the God who is within: within the reverberations of sound in the still centre. I shall continue to use all that comes to me, as part of a greater awareness and as a gifting of myself to the here and now. All that is in the present moment is the gift of God.

By about eleven o'clock I was so cold that I had to get up and go for a walk to warm my frozen feet. Heading out west in the direction of the blind lama's cave and tucking my binoculars into the top pocket of my anorak in case the cloud lifted, I made good progress and was pleased to discover that I do not get so breathless now on these slopes. I passed two areas with no bushes where an underground stream kept the soil moist. In this natural rock garden the large buttercup-yellow spurge was growing, with its red-veined leaves, dwarf mauve lupins with grey hairy leaves and stems, vivid tiny violets and small pale-blue gentians. Climbing higher I was watched by some dark bird of prey with shaggy-ended wings, circling on the thermals above my head. Then, as if this silent circling had been an instrumental cause, the sun came out behind the wings, silhouetting them like torn black pinions. I pressed on to the ridge above the lama's until, warm at last, I collapsed on the rough turf to enjoy the sunshine and the peace. On my way back I stopped again and leant on a rock and listened to the sound of the river far below me. The Bhute Kosi is constantly fed by melting snows so that it races fast through the gorges on a bed of large rocks and worn white stones. With my binoculars I could easily see the foamy blue-green water twisting its way through these boulders. The sound, from my high perch above the valley, was like the distant sound of the sea: an ever-present sound out of which the silence grew around me. Far below, on the other side of the river, two groups of stooping women were working in their stone-walled potato patches. Two butterflies, one two shades of orange and the other olive-green with brown-spotted wings, were enjoying the brief warmth on a neighbouring rock. I too enjoyed the rock's warmth against my back but, thinking of my sleeping-bag needing its airing and my still-damp clothes, I got up and wound my way back downhill to the sound of the warning cries of little wrens darting in and out of the flat juniper bushes and dwarf azaleas. On reaching the *gompa* I saw incense smoke was coming up through the boards on the floor of my cell and Norbu was still drumming rhythmically beneath me. Surely it must be a special day.

I had my lunch sitting on the rock behind the *gompa* admiring the work being done by Alison and others on the roof. Half of it is now resplendent with new paint. Below me, in a grassy cleft of the rock, is a beautiful large chalk-white anemone. All round me my personal paraphernalia is benefiting from the sun. No one seems to mind that I have taken over this rock. The lack of personal possessiveness is one of the most admirable things about this small community. I enjoyed my potato pancake with a thick vegetable sauce and a daub of yak butter. The physical comfort simply makes me feel more a part of everything which goes on around me. Norbu drums on. He must be quite hypnotized by the rhythm. It is certainly pounding through me and once or twice this morning I thought of the rhythmic beat of the Cherubim and Seraphim church in North Wharf Road, Paddington. It can put the mind to rest and free the emotions and spirit to soar; it can also put the mind to rest and leave the emotions open to manipulation. I want to live with my heart, but not without my head.

As I was finishing my lunch, cloud seemed to be coming up again. Alison, Merry and Drolkar had been joined by two lithe old Sherpas with bandy legs who have appeared to help with the work on the roof. Once they had begun, my way down the bank from my chosen rocky eyrie would have been barred. With my aired clothes and sleeping-bag and the remains of my lunch, therefore, I made my way past their ladders and up the steps to my cell, where, flopping on the bed, I fell asleep. I had been awake since 4:30, but even so I was amazed when I woke that I had managed to doze, sandwiched as I was between the religious chanting and throbbing below and the sandpapering, painting and resounding footsteps above. Later, when I returned my thermos and dinner plate to the kitchen, the two leather-coloured, bandy-legged mountain men were mending a large prayerwheel for Amala: the kind that turns in a box the size of a small cupboard and which she can work by pulling a string as she sits on her bed in the corner.

It is now 5pm, perhaps the hardest time of any day, when the clouds always seem to creep up on us as it gets dark. I sit in my small window to catch the last of the sun before it sinks in a pale misty glow behind Tangi Ragi Tau and before Alison brings my supper at around 7:30, by which time, if I am not unwell, I am always hungry. In front of me is my small shrine and I look at Tim's photograph of St Cuthbert's cross which he took on Lindisfarne lying in the ruins of the saint's cell on his smaller island. I read underneath the cross the words which were written by the Venerable Bede about Cuthbert, giving a sigh of relief and gratitude to be able to open my mind and heart to something so direct and simple:

> He was afire with heavenly love and devoted to unceasing prayer. He regarded the labour of helping the weaker brethren as the equivalent of prayer, remembering that he who said, "Thou shalt love the Lord thy God," also said, "Love thy neighbour."

Norbu has stopped at last in the *gompa* below. I have now found out that it was a monks' ceremony and that he had no one to share it with. This makes me sad and I wonder what the future can be for these small isolated monasteries. He must be exhausted and I am grateful for the silence after so much noise. Closing my eyes I listen to the distant surge of the river and hear the surge of the North Sea off the Northumberland coast. I remember how my husband Tim lay in the ruins of Cuthbert's cell, with the pink thrift in clumps among the stones around him and the gulls wheeling in the stormy sky. He recounted later —and this account is still kept on the island—of how he watched some dark clouds gathering behind the cross which seemed to symbolize the inner darkness of his cancer, his suffering and the clouded difficulty of letting go of all his anxieties and regrets. He felt the dark cloud of death hanging over his head. He lay there some time with closed eyes, then suddenly felt a warmth on his skin and looking up saw the clouds parting and the sun coming through to a bright patch of sky which left the cross silhouetted against the light. Then the clouds moved together again and were swept on by the wind. As usual he had his camera round his neck and was able to capture this moment of reassurance and hope. This picture, which I have in a small format before me, has been reproduced and used often. The story of it means a lot to me. He so loved life, but from that moment never clung to it.

Chapter 13

Towards the eastern *stupa*

Yes, it was a special preparation day yesterday for Nyung Na. As part of it Norbu and Anila had their heads close-shaved, but otherwise Anila took no part in it. I get the feeling that this is a pretty male-centred religion. The nuns are not treated with the same respect as the monks.

The small library here, which is next to the incense room, has a few books and pamphlets in English; otherwise the shelves are full of the beautiful rolled painted scroll-books of Tibet. At the moment there are few residents here who can read them. I have found a PhD thesis of an American anthropologist entitled *Sherpas through their Rituals*. In it the author describes the celebration of Nyung Na for the lay people as a rite of passage to post-parenthood. She writes that at the ceremonies she attended there were only the elderly of the village. She describes post-parenthood as a critical time in Sherpa life for, at the point when the youngest son is married, he inherits the family home and distributes the land among his siblings. The parents then experience a sense of rejection and loneliness and often actual poverty as they face death. Her interpretation centres round a period of liminality, symbolized by the three days in the *gompa* for the ceremonies—taking refuge in religion— to emerge with a greater sense of autonomy. This will in no way be the background for the young Western *dharma* students who manage to get up here in two weeks, but I suppose you could say that it will be a time of taking refuge in religion for them too—at least a time for further self-

awareness if not autonomy. Most of them will have made the primary
Buddhist commitment to "take refuge in the three jewels: Buddha,
dharma (doctrine) and *sangha* (community)." In addition there will be the
primary focus of this festival centred on attaining identification with
Chenrezi, the Buddha of Compassion. The three days of the ceremonies
are a withdrawal from the world for this purpose.

This morning I spent my meditation time lying on my stomach on
my bed because an old haemorrhoid problem has been troubling me
again. This has not been helped by sitting around on my hard window-
bench and on the rocks on the mountainside. I prayed in snatches of
remembered prayers leading into inner silence; letting the details and any
discomforts of the place fall away; being aware of the sounds of sanding
on the corrugated *gompa* roof still going on above me, but reaching back
into this quiet centre which I carry with me always. This is the place of
stillness in which I need the grace to gather and hold all experience in
balance and unity. After a long time of resting in this place I thought of
other remote places of silence and peace. My thoughts yesterday on
St Cuthbert's cross led me to Lindisfarne, and in my mind's eye I was
walking to the north end of the island down the green lane where the
gnarled hawthorns with flat tops all lean together away from the wind.
Between these twisted trees and the grey stone wall which marks the
grazing limit for the sheep, the lapwings are calling, tumbling and
rejoicing in the May wind, a salt-laden May wind which tingles on your
skin—so different from the May wind here, which swirls the cloud up
towards the snow line, propelled by the warm air from the valley below,
unwrapping, as it goes, the clinging damp of the night.

In the sunshine and wind from the sea of Lindisfarne I walked, in my
mind, past the ponds in the dunes, surrounded by small violets that are the
same colour as those beside the paths here, and watched the newts dart in
and out among the moss. Then coming to the rocky cliffs of a northeast
bay, I lay in a curved arm of the shore, sheltering from the wind and pressing my back against the sandy marram grass and my feet against a warm
rock, watching the sea. Then, still in my imagination, I walked back round
the shore to St Cuthbert's cell, past the families of eider duck rising towards
me on the crests of the waves, then falling back invisible into a trough
while the herring gulls and black-backs wheeled and cried round my head.

Cuthbert had two cells: the one where the cross is, near the abbey ruins on Holy Island, and one on the Outer Farnes, where he was happiest. But the way his compassion moved him was that he repeatedly responded to "the weaker brethren" by leaving these beloved cells and his conversations with the seals and sea-birds, to return to responsibility in the world, sometimes to sort out problems in one of the Border abbeys, sometimes to conduct missions and finally to be consecrated Bishop of Durham. This was his cross, the substance of his offering. "Being afire with heavenly love" for him did not permit complete withdrawal because of his compassion for his neighbour in the world. There are a number of temporary hermit figures around here: Losang (American monk, Richard) in one of the lower cells; Michael, an Australian, in the well-built and beautifully sited top cell. When out on that stretch of the mountain I can hear his radio playing from time to time. These rarely glimpsed characters are in addition to Merry and Harry over by the blind Cherok Lama. A hermit's life, as my hermit friend Sister Eileen Mary told me, should help the solitary to achieve greater simplicity. The renunciation is not punitive, but allowing nothing to get in the way. Here, as on Bardsey Island, where I met her, it is taken for granted that you trust people. Nothing is locked up. Honesty is the climate in which all relate, for all are interdependent in this remote region, as they are on that other beautiful island in the Atlantic where the Celtic hermits lived. Perhaps Michael is not quite so happy with the silence, because in addition to hearing his radio from time to time I also encounter him in the kitchen talking to Anila. I too much enjoy Anila's company, but I would hate to have a radio. It would feel like an intrusion on that special slice of time, which is already slipping by so fast; it would get in the way.

I keep being struck by contrasts here—or perhaps it is only my culture-bound way of looking at things which prevents me from seeing the similarities. The Buddhist sage Milarepa, whom I knew of but had not read before, nine centuries ago described all human relationships as worthless. All worldly pursuits ended in sorrow, he said, therefore as life is short and the time of death is uncertain, it is better to withdraw and apply yourself to meditation. For the Tibetan Buddhist ideal, as expressed in its monasticism, seems to be to separate yourself from the world *because* it is worthless. I feel the ideal has not the same root in most Christian monasticism, where withdrawal is for silence, stability and prayer rather than because the world, though containing evil, is of no account. The Celtic hermit tradition was rooted in the God-revealing beauty of nature. Even some of the desert Fathers and Mothers, when sought by would-be disciples, were discovered on their way back to the world. Meditation and self-knowledge are common to both religious traditions, but the processes of self-knowledge are better understood in Buddhist practice. Here Christians have so much to learn, as well as much to share. Allowing compassion for ourselves is so often forgotten in Christianity and is a practice Buddhists can help us understand. But I have found no counterpart in any Buddhist literature of Cuthbert's love of, and identification with, the natural world. For Buddhists it is part of illusory objectivity: therefore, presumably, there is no merit in spending time on it. The divine is only within.

This afternoon I went for a walk towards the eastern *stupa*. This is the tomb of one of the previous Lawudo Lamas. I originally set out just to take exercise and to keep warm but quickly regretted having neither my binoculars nor my camera with me. In one of the clearings among the low juniper and rhododendron bushes I saw a whole family of blood-pheasants—*chilme* in Nepalese. They seem quite tame, making little *chirk-chirk* noises to each other as in a family group they move around in the scrub looking for food. Whenever I have observed them they have not been alarmed enough to take flight so I have not seen properly, the male's blood-red tail feathers, but you can glimpse them and his red legs, as he pecks around. Quite soon I encountered a pair of collared grosbeaks sitting on the top of a tree. As they saw me and took off, their bright yellow bodies were clear against the dark foliage. The wind had dropped since the morning and it was warm enough to linger and watch things that moved. Below me, over the miniature Mende fields, the clouds were still hovering. Above, as I looked to the ridge, was the dark silhouette of a large eagle of some kind. I tried to keep it in sight as my path rose towards the *stupa* but small trees kept coming between us. By the time I had reached the crumbling stone monument the ridge behind was completely swathed in cloud and the fields below were in a patch of sunlight. The movements of sun and cloud change so quickly here. No wonder they say at Lawudo not to go too far without warning them.

I sat on the ledge of the *stupa* facing south, soaking in the landscape and feeling the fragments of ancient yellow stone rough beneath me, when, with much croaking, I was completely surrounded in a swirl of choughs. I love these birds. When I was down in the lower cell a pair of them woke me in the morning with their cry, quite like that of the ravens, and I opened my door to look at them. They were close in front of me and did not stop pecking for grubs in the damp ground with their curved red beaks or moving their elegant red legs in a rather disdainful way. Around me now, at the *stupa*, they sauntered and pecked, occasionally stopping to clean both sides of their beaks against a rock. I could hear the loud whistle of a sibia, but as at Kopan, never managed to see it. On my way back, however, I identified a pair of scarlet minavets feeding on seeds of clematis. As I returned to the spot where I had seen the blood pheasants, a majestic monal, the national bird of Nepal, was sitting on a rock cleaning his wing feathers, quite close to the twisty path. His mate was on the ground beside him and soon another cock came in sight. I have never before seen these most splendid birds: about the size of a small peacock, with a similar feathered tuft on the head and the same iridescent blue on their massive wings. When something disturbed them —it did not seem to be the sight of me—they took off, the males displaying their flashy golden tail feathers and wing tips. I stayed sitting in this mountain rock-garden among the clumps of tiny violets and the yellow spurge, thinking about the philosophical proposition which is basic to Buddhism: that all this is illusion. I remember, when Alison was living with me in my London house, having a conversation with her on the stairs—which was the usual place for our unplanned and most profound conversations. She repeated this proposition to me and I could not help telling her about G. E. Moore, who, while having breakfast in Cambridge, countered it by banging hard on the table and saying something to the effect that this table may be an illusion but he knew it was real because when he hit it, it hurt. I know that all this diversity and beauty brings to me, through my senses, an almost unbearable feeling of wonder and joy which almost hurts, an unrepeatable experience of reality. I don't mind that I have forgotten the gadgets—camera and binoculars—that help me record, categorize and define it all. I have simply *been* with it in the short space of this afternoon. "Not how the world is, but *that* it is, is the mystery"—my favourite quote from Wittgenstein! But mystery is not the same thing as illusion.

I learnt this evening that the tiered levels of a *stupa* are symbols of the Buddhist way, mounting ever higher and narrower to the final enlightenment. I am reminded of the Ascension, which is today. I must not start thinking of this odd experience of Jesus's disciples in this setting, because it gets me back into the wrong model—of exterior events. I need to shift the boundaries, though the curiously different ways our two traditions have developed makes a more flexible understanding difficult, and seems to keep the boundaries in place. Christians talk of an incarnate God while the Buddhists talk of a fully Enlightened Being. This difference in language and perception clearly represents a different awareness of the movements of grace—or increasing enlightenment. For Christians there is the transcendent God manifest in humanity, representing the highest human goal. For Buddhists there is a man who achieves the highest human goal, enlightenment, which enables him to transcend his humanity, who is then treated like a God. There is more difference in language and symbol than in process. How fettered and bound we all are by the limitations of our language and cultural conditioning—as I keep reminding myself. Whichever movement we feel a part of, as we experience this paradox it speaks to us of the same human goal. For there is no doubt that many guru figures have been so full of the spirit that to their disciples they have seemed more than human. I do not want to make comparisons. I need to stay with my own uncertainty about all this—without judgement. It is enough that all the major religions of the world have sprung from their founder's influence on their friends and followers and that they have lasted as they have and become the vehicles of so much spiritual search and endeavour. None of the major religions are now restricted to the cultures from which they sprang and for all, this is the challenge of the twenty-first century.

Chapter 14

Tsampa for breakfast

Tsampa again for breakfast. I am not sure how ready I would be to eat it except near the borders of Tibet. The Tibetans came across last week to Thame, which is the last village you can get a trekking permit to. The valley, as it turns north after that, goes directly up to the border. Norbu went down with the yak to get a sack of *tsampa*. It is barley flour which has gone through several processes, including soaking, baking and grinding. It is like dark brown coarse sand. You eat it hot with a daub of yak butter on top, made into a paste of whatever thickness you like by adding hot black Tibetan tea. You play sand-castles in your bowl with it, adding more tea as needed, for it can soak up an enormous amount of liquid. I eat it here with thankfulness as it is a great way to keep warm and gain energy. I have just finished mine, sitting on the window seat in my cell looking across the juniper bushes festooned with budding white clematis montana to the western *stupa* ridge. Beyond that the mountains are lost in cloud. There is still some hot weak black tea in the thermos beside me with which I shall end my breakfast. This is even more of a thermos culture than the Chinese—though all the thermo flasks you can buy are made in China. Every bit of boiled water is saved in them to retain the heat. Anila has a range of thermoses on her shelf in the kitchen. In one big one she will have "Sherpa tea" made with sugar and yak milk and in another black tea. Boiled water for drinking is kept in the others, which are replenished from the pot on the fire. Each hermit is taken a freshly filled thermos of the tea of his choice with each meal. These are carried to them with their food by either Norbu or Drolkar. When I go down to the kitchen to fetch my own food I sit by the fire as Anila finishes the cooking and wait while she fills the bowls to be taken to the hermits. This is the time when we chat about what is happening in this small community—about Amala's health, the dzo which did not return from the mountain last night or the plans she has to work in the *gompa* fields tomorrow. She gives me my tin mug filled with black tea and I warm my hands round it as we talk. For her I can see that mine seems a rather relaxed form of retreat but it builds up a good form of friendship!

In the evenings I get into my sleeping-bag at about seven o'clock, by which time it is quite dark and I need to do this to keep warm. I light my small candle and read by its light until Alison or Drolkar bring my supper. Drolkar seems to have taken this on because it has become her time when we two can talk in greater privacy than in the kitchen. She does not leave my bowl and thermos outside the door as she does for the hermits, but, often singing as she comes up the back steps, she pushes open my door and comes into the room. Sometimes she sits on my bed and haltingly answers my questions about her family, especially her sisters whose companionship she clearly misses. Alison is teaching her English and she is getting pretty good at expressing herself. Sometimes she looks at the pictures forming my primitive shrine and often she wanders about picking up the things which interest her, turning them over in the darkness and asking questions. "What this for?" "To put on face in sun." "What this?" "For quick cleaning when no water," etc. Last night she took my candle over to the pictures and peered carefully at them. "Mother— baby?" "Yes, copy of old picture. You like baby to love?" "Yes, me baby. Anila no baby—nun. Me first house then baby." She has got it worked out. She picks up my wooden hand cross. "This cross?" "Yes, good to hold, good to feel." She holds it against her cheek, then smiles and puts it down. Yesterday evening, after more looking around she began to whistle under her breath. When she does this, or begins to sing, I know she is on the move. I can often hear her on the mountainside long before I can see her. She is happy when she is on the move. She moves out of my door into the darkness saying "goodnight" and leaving me to my thick noodle soup in which chopped spinach, preserved in brine, is floating about.

She works hard and is more mature than a Western child of her age. She laughs with Anila as she washes the dishes in the minimum amount of water. She also fetches the water every day from the pipe stuck into the spring a quarter of a mile away, carrying it on her back in two big plastic cans. When Anila thwarts some plan of hers, however, she develops a threatening sulky look and whistles and sings no more. She seems to be really happiest when she is calling in the dzos and calves for milking and feeding. She sometimes has to go miles up and down these rough tracks to find them. As they eat all the plant shoots and erode the steep slopes with their hooves, they have to go further and further away to find enough food. She loves the shaggy-coated dzo calves, one brown-and-white and the other black. They have pieces of coloured tape tied into their ears to identify them when they stray. If Anila is busy Drolkar milks the two lactating dzos, who produce a very small amount of milk. After this she feeds the old pack yak and the other dzo, with any remains of food from the kitchen. This is all chucked into a large can and, with a few potatoes added, is stewed every afternoon on the fire. Nothing is wasted and it reminds me of wartime at home. We used to cook all our kitchen scraps overnight in a great iron pot in the bottom of the Aga. My oldest son Toby's first responsibility, as a small boy when he got back from school, was to take this evil-smelling brew out to the garden shed, mix it with what was euphemistically called "balancer meal"—for which we had sacrificed our egg coupons—and then feed the results to the chickens. Fifty years later he still remembers the foul smell and the no-waste routine. Drolkar's last task, as darkness falls, is to shut the double wooden doors leading from the main path into the courtyard, to secure all the animals there for the night.

During my meditation this morning I spent some time looking at my rough card of the ikon of Our Lady of Zigorsk. This ikon form, showing the head and shoulders of Mary, with the baby's head bent rather unnaturally back from his neck so that his cheek can rest against his mother's face, is called a Mother of God of Tenderness. The child's left hand is in the folds of her veil and her eyes look beyond him to the world. This Mother of God of Tenderness, of compassion, we might say, is for all creatures. Mary has always been a model of compassion for Christians, but I do not see her as a model of passivity, any more than I feel that Chenrezi is intended to exemplify a purely interior attitude. I read the *Magnificat*. Mary's response to the angel seems neither fearful or anxious but assured and joyful. It appears possible for her not only to link this message directly to the Messianic prophecies, but also to a sense of fulfilment for herself. The advent of this child becomes part of the vision she has about the social issues which are important for her. "He hath filled the hungry with good things and the rich he hath sent empty away." She expressed her dependence on God, but Mary was no simple pious girl thinking of personal holiness, as some ikons, prayers and other aspects of Mariology have sought to make her.

My mother, who was always a bit disturbed by my interest in religion, made me laugh once about the *Magnificat*. She had been educated in a Roman Catholic convent and the standard of piety and caring which she encountered there never really left her as a possible ideal, but intellectually she went along with my father's agnosticism. Sometimes she read the Bible. On this occasion I was staying with my family and went into her bedroom to say goodnight. In an angry voice she said, "I've been reading the *Magnificat*. No wonder Jesus was a crypto-communist: he got it from his mother. Where did she get it from, do you think?" "The Old Testament prophets, I should think," I replied; "they were a pretty revolutionary lot." This conversation took place in the early days of the Cold War, when everyone was looking for reds under the beds. As the good Conservative my mother was, she wanted to keep Mary in the convent; but for me it is important that Mary looks beyond the child, as in this ikon, to the world. I think the Buddha of compassion also needs to look—with all his many eyes—more deeply into the world. When I leave I shall give my little card of Our Lady of Zigorsk to Drolkar.

On my morning walk one or two of the spectacular black-and-yellow finches came diving down the slope so close to my head that I felt the movement of the air. They were larger than the grosbeaks I see in the trees and clearly were not used to humans. I also saw a bird I have wanted to see for some time, for I have often heard it. Its call is *titu, titu*, and that is its name in Nepali. By this call I located it busy eating the seeds of the juniper: a small pink rosefinch, which also sucks the nectar from the rhododendron and azalea flowers. But it is shy and flew off as I approached. About the same size, but less shy, was a small yellow-and-green warbler—I think the grey-hooded—hovering in the bushes catching insects. My most exciting encounter today, however, was a large male blood-pheasant at very close range, which seemed quite undisturbed by me: its back and wing feathers were a kind of dappled grey, shading to yellow and grey on its breast. It has a red eye-stripe and feathered comb and in addition to its brilliant tail feathers has bright red legs—a lot of startling blood colour, in fact.

Merry appeared while I was having a warm-up at the kitchen fire before lunch. She confirmed much of what I had learnt in *Sherpas through their Rituals* about the condition of some older people. I suppose even minimal medical advances have prolonged their lives, and couples with young families will give the children preference when food is scarce or conditions hard. She says that the independent, individualistic nature of Sherpa society does not engender a sense of community responsibility for the old, and she told me about two old single women who had died on their own, near the blind lama's cave. I think Alison does not like Merry discussing this kind of thing with me, as she is still so uncritical of all that goes on here. Tonight as I sat on my bed waiting for Alison or Drolkar to bring me my supper, I did not even bother to light my candle but sat in darkness. Silence and *folded* hands—drawing my energy to my centre—in the stillness. This is a silence which sifts and allows what is of no importance to flow away: around me the "noiseless solitude" which Milarepa says "is guide to lasting contemplation". This contemplation, this thanksgiving, seems then to well up from deep inside me. Silence and *open* hands—holding an open heart—open to everything: without trying to intellectualize and explain to myself perception and seeing: gifting myself to the unknown, the darkness, the silence.

Chapter 15

Emptiness and silence

Saturday 26 May

I had an upset stomach last night so I had no supper and in consequence was pretty breathless by the early hours. It is strange how this altitude problem is kept at bay by food and drink. However, I had hot water in my thermos which kept me going, and I found my breathing easier if I propped myself up against the wall and put my anorak round my shoulders to keep warm. Eventually I slept quite well in this position for a couple of hours or more. Alison popped her head in to see how I was and then kindly fetched my breakfast. She is thoughtfully finding a middle path between taking care of me and not invading my space or my times of silence. It was certainly good not to have to struggle with the damp and cold before having something to eat, and it enabled me to have my meditation period in my sleeping-bag. I am still in it now at 9:15 and it looks as if the sun is breaking through.

   I often begin my meditations by humming or singing one of the Taizé chants. I like the sound in my *gompa* cell and I feel connected with all those groups of people with whom I have sung them before or who may be singing them now—though I must say my voice this morning

• Beyond Phakding

overleaf: *• The first sight of Lawudo (centre), Mount Kapsale behind (18,612ft)*
• Lawudo: The courtyard, with the gompa on the right

sounds pretty weak and cracked. Because I have been dwelling on the idea of guru-devotion I thought also of the song *Guru Jesus*. Humming this brought to my mind my own personal image of him: not the blond Anglo-Saxon in the white nightie looking down at me as a child from the picture of *All Things Bright and Beautiful* on the nursery wall, but a sparse Galilean, such as I saw in that country in the early 1970s. The image had been with me, however, long before that time, but being in the place and seeing how close it was to the real appearance of the local people strengthened it for me. As I see him he is always some distance ahead of me climbing a fairly steep mountain path and encouraging, even beckoning, me on. His feet are often quite clear to me but I never seem to see his face. I worked quite a lot with this image of "guru-Jesus" when doing a retreat in daily life with a Jesuit and it has come back quite strongly to me on these precipitous mountain tracks. This Jesus is more like the poor monk Norbu, whose shoes are nearly worn out and who set out at first light, with the yak, to walk down to Namche market and back; more like this Sherpa man so deeply involved in the daily struggle than the Buddha of Compassion portrayed in the *thangka* above my bed with his impassive body decked in jewels and his pale white feet with their untrodden soles turned upwards in the full lotus position.

Though I have tried to resist the urge to dip into the few English-language books about Buddhism in the library here, I have read some of John Blofield's book *Beyond the Gods*. In this he writes about the personification of "wisdom-energies" and the different ways "Buddha aspects" are understood in different Buddhist traditions. I hope to try to keep away from the interior mental arguments which meditating on these questions brings on in me: guardian deities versus Buddha aspects, speculations on the similarities and differences in Christian and Buddhist use of symbols and so on—interior chatter without end! I think I must be content with Blofield's first explanation of wisdom-energies, interpreting them, as far as I can, through Jung's archetypes. For, as Jung says, archetypes are analogous to instincts—dynamic forces in the human personality. What I do find it hard to come to terms with is this

• *Lawudo: Yak eating hay outside the stable*
• *Mende fields below the courtyard*

emphasis on all objective experience being an illusion. Is it this which leads to the need to concretize these aspects or instincts into objects of veneration? No, I think I must shift that standpoint also because, at what Buddhists would call a "skilful" level, such objects are only a focus for meditation, as the statue of a saint can be in Christianity. Behind all my questioning is my sense that in the process of acquiring selflessness the Buddhist way is inward-turning and self-regarding. However, at the same time it is deeply serious about the spiritual search for a transcending unity. Only the mystical tradition within Christianity is concerned or serious about this.

Sunday 27 May

I ate very little yesterday. After a promising start the day was quite awfully wet and cold. On returning from Namche, Norbu lent me a splendid pair of Chinese trousers of an unbleached cotton material, woven so that they were all shaggy inside like sheepskin. As it was too wet to go far outside I had to sit in my room and they proved wonderfully warm worn over my own trousers. Alison has been busy over Merry's coming birthday and the preparations for the arrival of a Spanish nun.

I was led by some of my reading to meditate on emptiness. This is a good setting. Inside, I am literally rather empty and if I look out of my window I know that, outside, the slopes of Kapsale rise above me almost empty of human life. The immediate *gompa* scene is also emptied today of any familiar detail by the opaqueness of the surrounding cloud. Here, for me in my cell, are none of the props we build around ourselves to give us our supposed sense of identity and completeness. Possessions, status, friends, achievements are merely empty notions here. I realize how quickly we become identified with our possessions to the point where they possess us. Here I have very few belongings and am attached to nothing which gives me status. The only things I belong to are the fleas that eat me every night. This experience of my emptiness joins me more intimately to the few I share it with, who give me my only sense of "being" moment by moment. I stayed with this non-person, neither reading nor writing, but just looking out of the window into the surrounding clouds. Should I actually need to get away this thick cloud would now make it impossible. I felt sad and vulnerable but also elated to be, so to speak, within myself, part of this great high wilderness. There is something almost holy, but also humbling, about responding to the challenge of an environment such as this and embracing it as an aspect of self-emptying.

Milarepa said, "Just as a starving man cannot be fed by the knowledge of food, but needs to eat, so we too need to experience in meditation the meaning of emptiness." The high places as well as the wilderness are within. Acknowledging the powerlessness and the emptiness in my situation seems also to be a part of what Buddhists call "mindfulness". Jung says somewhere that in psychology you possess nothing unless you have experienced it in reality. I have so often, in my imagination, tried to experience the things I experience here, as I have also tried to imagine various emotions and states of mind to enable me to get alongside people I am trying to help. Equally often I am good at fending off realities I do not want to experience because they might be painful. Here there has been no escape. I am moved by my realization that the emptiness for me is part of my letting go of my ideas of God.

At midday I went down to the kitchen to ask Anila for plain potatoes for lunch. She greeted me as usual: "Ah, Pen." Then anxiously: "So sorry." Patting my stomach I said, "No worry, getting better." "Sit, sit," she pointed to the bench by the fire. I moved towards the warmth. "Special," she said and put into my hand a small hard-boiled egg. I bowed and accepted it quite touched by her thoughtfulness. Eggs are a luxury up here and are usually eaten as an omelette or fried on top of a griddle-bread. "For lunch, please," I said, "just one or two plain potatoes." She took three from the big pot of cooked ones standing on the top of the clay stove and put them in the embers to toast for me. As each one browned she took them from the fire, rubbed them in her hands and gave them to me with such pride and courtesy they might have been diamonds. "Stay, Pen, stay eat." So instead of returning to my room I sat with her in the smoke and watched her prepare the food for everyone else. She is a remarkable woman, the eldest of Amala's three children. Lama Zopa is in the middle. She has lived here all her life and for the last twenty-six years has been cooking and caring for her mother and all who come to the *gompa*, from Norbu to the youngest Western visitor. She is also responsible for the animals and the garden as well as going quite often to cultivate the *gompa* fields, as far off as Thame. She is short and shapeless, with a rather thick-skinned worn face which crumples up humorously when she laughs. On her head she wears an old russet-red woollen hat like a tea-cosy. Her other clothes, which may have started this russet colour, are now shades darker from grime and smoke. On top, over her robe, she wears a cardigan tucked into the sash round her waist and, in addition, the padded protective kidney-warmer tied around her back. Finally there is an ancient piece of flowered material tucked into her front, which serves as an apron. When she cooks, she rubs her fingers on this frayed apron and goes on doling out the rice into the bowls with her hands. Then stretching over from her yakskin seat on the floor she feeds the fire with dung. What matter hygiene? What I appreciate is her warm heart.

The paradoxes of life in this place keep surfacing. It is quite extraordinary to think that many people here have never seen a wheeled vehicle, not even a bicycle, much less a car or a train, for the ground is so steep and rocky that no carts of any kind are used. We are in fact about ten days' walk from the nearest road. Yet over towards the Rowaling valley some attempts at a hydro-electric project are under way. The first early efforts were ruined by the Chinese, whose undertakings of the same nature in Tibet ended in a burst dam which caused floods and devastation right through this region. However, we hear blastings in the mountains from time to time and with my binoculars I can see the buildings of a new depot up behind Thame where the large sections of piping are being stored. These sections appear to be about eight feet by three feet and two of them at a time are brought up from the Lukla airstrip by four men, each with a weight-carrying leather band around his forehead with two sections of pipe slung in a cradle between them.

After lunch the cloud lifted so I went for a walk towards the Cherok caves. I saw brown fronds of bracken uncurling and a small brilliant yellow potentilla, neither of which I had seen before. Also on my path was a large pile of faeces not unlike a guinea-pig's. I think it must be pika, for they seem about guinea-pig size, but I could find no hole or burrow anywhere near. The only suspected pika habitation I have found is a hole going well back into the bank by the lower cells, but there is no sign there of any droppings. Perhaps pika are very hygienic creatures and keep these well away from their burrows.

While sitting on some juniper scrub to keep off the damp I thought about the different qualities of the silences in this place. Yesterday I spent all day in my cell and at one point in the afternoon the silence was so profound, seemingly so contained within the wooden building, that as I looked out at the cloud which pressed around us I might have been the only person in the whole of Solu Khumbu. This exterior shrouded silence in the *gompa* leads to an inner reflective state where I can wander in my mind without a focus or any sense of time, and it is enhanced in the building by the pervading smell of drying incense. In the attic above my cell the sprigs of incense plant are laid out to dry. This smell and the associations of prayer and curling smoke add to my sense of wandering without purpose, in a mental landscape with no clarity. Out on the mountainside the smell of crushed juniper beneath me has some of the same qualities because juniper is also burnt in the large incense burners out in the open. Here, however, all silence has the background roar of the river crashing over the boulders below and a quality of the light which is apparent whenever the sun shines through the cloud. It is a quality of clarity which affects my mind as well as my sight and which lends to silence a different kind of depth from the shrouded silence of the clouds. To anything I hear within this silence there is a special depth and brilliance. I am alert for all the little bird calls and animal movements as I go out into my senses of sight, smell and hearing which I hope to lead me to the reality behind all this diversity. Sometimes one of the tiny warblers sings a limpid series of notes into the great empty valley and the final soundwave hangs in the air above the river's roar, while a deep, wide silence breaks over me as the last note fades into the vast spaces. This is the sort of silence which I become part of in such a different way from in my cell: a silence which flows out and encircles all the world, silence like a music which contains all sounds.

Chapter 16

Washing at the water pipe

Monday 28 May

I got up at 5:30 this morning as the sunrise, in great splendour, caught all the peaks of Kwangde and Tangi Ragi Tau with orange light. So often days seem to start like this and then by about 9:30 we are overtaken by the cloud again. Pulling on my trousers and anorak over my night things, and armed with my camera, I spent an hour wandering up and down the many levels of the immediate *gompa* area, taking pictures of these great dazzling peaks as they emerged from the dark shadows of the valleys. I stood on the wall below my cell and, as nearly as possible from the same spot, took three shots across the whole Kwangde range from east to west. If it comes out it should be a good panoramic reminder of the grandeur of these peaks. The rising sun was at such an angle that the gorges made by the movement of the glaciers in the winter stood out like black scars against the vivid white and golden snow.

One portrait I achieved which I have been trying to get for some time was of the raven with the pink Buddhist tie! This creature once invaded the kitchen when the door had been left open, and took some food. Norbu left the door open again and lay in wait with a piece of blessed pink cloth. He caught the bird and tied this round his neck. Lots of people would have wrung its neck instead, but Norbu is a good Buddhist and this bird and his mate—nicknamed Bliss and Void by Alison—are familiars of the place. Their territory seems to be the area between the *gompa* and the eastern *stupa*. Whenever I go in that direction they follow me closely, perching near at hand when I sit and hoping that I have a snack with me to share with them, which is not often. Today Bliss was greeting the morning on the courtyard wall with his head held high above his pink insignia. He was completely in possession of the place.

During a short teatime conversation round the fire yesterday with Anila, Alison said (in the special voice she has for talking about him), "Lama Zopa says, 'All problems come from "I"—"I" wanting, wanting, wanting. No wanting—no problems.'" Well, you do not need to climb to 12,500 feet to discover that, I thought to myself, and then felt a bit mean because she is so open and friendly and, in many ways, naive. Thinking about it afterwards I realized that when up here she completely absorbs the cultural and religious assumptions relating to a *rinpoche*, while I, in sceptical fashion, remain equally absorbed by my cultural assumptions. The result is that with her I am often in my "comparative-studies mode" and if I am needing to return to my silence, we end up by merely exchanging clichés.

The sun persisted all day. After putting my flea-bag and night clothes on the back rock to air, I put all my washing requirements for body, hair and clothes, plus a drink and one of the last of my crunchy bars, into my small backpack and with all my dirty clothes in my bucket I walked down the path towards the water pipe. On my way I met an old mountain man—a Tibetan from the Khampa district in the northeast— coming up towards Lawudo. His hair was in a long pigtail at the back, plaited with coloured material, a turquoise stone in his left ear, and across his shoulders an old yakskin coat. His trousers were worn and tucked into odd-coloured socks. His ragged boots were of red felt. I was resting on a stone as he came up towards me and he sat down beside me as I smiled and said my *namaste*. After looking me over in silence for some time he bent down and touched my boots. I pointed to his and said "good". He made a movement of hands in the direction of mine, implying "strong". "English," I said and then, with gestures and grimaces of his lined face, he suggested we swap. "Stay Lawudo," I said; "Must get back Kathmandu. No boots, no good." Then I pointed to my bucket and in the direction of the pipe. We got up and parted amicably though I felt sad I had nothing to give him, as I feared if I shared my crunchy bar I might never lose him and a good wash would prove impossible. On my return to the *gompa* he was in close conversation in the corner of the big room with Amala, apparently an old Tibetan trader friend of hers. He smiled and almost winked at me, pointing to his boots as I bowed and went past the door on my way to get my lunch.

My ablutions were marvellous. The sun was getting quite hot. Descending into the shallow stream which runs constantly from the spring into which the pipe is stuck, I filled my bucket. Then I stripped and soaped myself all over, keeping an eye out for any other mountain men that might be coming up the path! I rinsed by pouring another bucket of water over myself, all the time relishing the soft cold water on my wretchedly inflamed fleabites. Then with only my towel round my waist, in more fresh water, I washed my hair and sprayed it direct from the pipe. So close to the snowline the water certainly felt terribly cold on my head, but it was my first decent wash for a couple of weeks and a delightfully invigorating one. I then soaked my clothes in the bucket, put on pants and T-shirt and had my drink and snack. Several pairs of bright orange butterflies were hovering about and a stonechat was dipping and calling above me. Only small wispy clouds were hovering round the highest peaks, as I got my clothes washed and hung on the bushes to dry. As visibility was so good I rather regretted having lent my binoculars to Norbu but was content to lie back and relax in the sun.

Tuesday 29 May

It is 2:30 in the morning. I am having a wakeful rather breathless night. I think this is probably because I have not eaten enough for the last two days. Since the last bout of indigestion, which was also suffered by others, due we think to some undercooked type of small bean, the heavy food has been difficult for me to cope with. I must make an effort today to eat a bit more. During this sleeplessness I have been trying to recall prayers and collects that I used to be able to reel off by heart. On Sundays, at my Anglican boarding school, we had to learn the collect for the day before we could write a letter home, then getting into a "crocodile" walk to matins at the village church.

Instead I say to myself: "O Thou who sendest forth the light,

createst the morning, makest the sun to shine on the good and on the
evil; lift Thou up the light of Thy countenance upon us, enlighten our
minds with the knowledge of Thy truth; that in Thy light we may see the
light and at the last, through the light of grace, the light of glory." I
wonder if I have remembered it correctly? I don't think I had read this
beautiful morning prayer of Lancelot Andrews when I was at school. I
came across the *Preces Privatae* in the 1940s and this has been in my head
ever since. It came to my mind for two reasons this morning: first
because I am waiting for the light of dawn to show in my window, and
second because the other word which keeps on revolving in my mind in
this Buddhist environment, after *compassion*, is *enlightenment*. The Christian
emphasis on Christ as the light of the world is brought together by
Lancelot Andrews with the "light which createst the morning" from
Genesis. This light is for me a sign of the original blessing of creation—
something in which all creation partakes and a symbol of humanity's
hope in the gift of enlightenment at the end of all journeys and
searching. It seems to me that, during the search, such an enlightenment
comes not only through the enlightened mind, but often through a flash,
or "blick" as Ian Ramsey called it, of awareness or unmerited grace. Two
aspects of this way of understanding enlightenment are inimical to
Buddhism, first of all because anything unmerited goes against the
doctrine of *karma* and secondly, but interwoven with it, is that this
original creative light implies some form of theism. For me it brings
prayer and meditation out of the limited world of introspection, ethical
choices and self-improvement, into a greater involvement with all that *IS*.
Perhaps the search itself is all the enlightenment we will ever get.

The other recurring word in my thoughts is still compassion and I
have been comparing it with the word we have so distorted in English—
charity. "O Lord, who hast taught us that all our doings without charity
are nothing worth ... send into our hearts ..." That is not quite right and I
cannot go any further. This experience, in a strange land, of feeling cut
off from so much in the way of references to which I would normally
have access is my own fault, the working of my *karma*. I do not often use
an office book or any book of formal prayers, so I decided to bring
nothing like that with me. But I have lived with the assumption of being
able to turn to them when I wanted. I am regretting my decision and

shall return to them thirsty, as one who has been a long journey in a dry land.

It is raining again outside and the light has not yet come up from behind Khumbila. I write with my right hand and hold my small candle steady on its piece of Himalayan rock with my left. The quality of the candlewax is unreliable and every now and again it splutters and nearly goes out. Let there be light—especially as the Chinese bulb which Norbu bought for me in the market on Saturday has already given up on my torch! Sometime soon the pale light will begin to show up the wooden cross-bars of my little window. It reminds me of the ways of meditating which Tim developed when he had to lie flat on his back and such simple ordinary things became creative catalysts for him. Sometime before the bars are clearly defined I shall hear the tinkle of the bell round the neck of the senior dzo as she leads the rest of the mixed herd back to the courtyard after they have had a night on the mountain. This happens when there has not been much food to give them the evening before but it only compounds the problem, for in addition to eating all the grass and small bushes that might retain the topsoil, the animals' hooves so churn it up that with the next heavy rains it will be swept into the valley.

I saw the same thing happening in New Caledonia in opposite climatic conditions on the Pacific rim. There the native Kanak people, who are not allowed by the French to own cattle, have a well-balanced agriculture of vegetables, pigs and chickens interspersed with the great forest trees in their reserves on the northeast side of the island. On the west side, in the areas given to the French ex-convicts who were allowed to import cattle from France, the over-grazing and the soil erosion are far worse than they are here. The only plant left growing on the hillsides in the dry season is the pink and yellow lantana, which no animal will eat. I could see this attractive bush growing all round Kopan where, for this reason, it is used to make hedges. Here in Lawudo, they get only about a litre a day in milk from each of the milking dzos. In the miles they walk in search of food the tough creatures must burn up any benefit they get from it, with little energy to spare for lactation. As none of the bull calves or any of the herd will be killed for meat I cannot see why they keep them. Calling them in, milking and feeding them takes at least two hours of Drolkar's time twice a day, but she loves the calves, especially the little black one. Soon I shall hear her singing as she opens the courtyard gate for them and squats down on a damp stone to milk the dzos in the early light.

Yaks and dzos are not the only cause of soil erosion on these high slopes. Every Sherpa home has a wood-burning cooking fire. These people have to go higher and higher up the mountains to cut wood. In this whole area of the National Park it is supposed to be illegal to cut wood, so some of the climbing may be to avoid the authorities—but how could they possibly keep watch in all these remote valleys or prosecute such poor people who have absolutely no alternative source of energy or warmth? In the meantime from all the slopes in the Solu Khumbu and from all the south-facing valleys in Tibet, the fertile topsoil of the Himalayas is being swept into the Bay of Bengal, causing appalling flooding on the way, especially in Bangladesh.

Only the drumming of the rain on the newly painted corrugated-iron roof, the occasional spluttering of my candle and the rhythmic snores of Norbu in the *gompa* below me break into the almost palpable, incense-laden, enclosed silence of these wooden walls which hold in the dark remnant of the night and hold out the threatening sense of the high snows. Before my candle finally went out the window bars were framing the grey light of dawn reflected off the peaks of Kwangde. I slept at last and dreamt of my sisters.

Chapter 17

Prayerwheels and mantras

At 11:30am I went down into the *gompa* to meditate for half an hour before lunch. I had hoped to have the place to myself but the old lady was there murmuring her prayers and bowing to the profusion of images. The effect of all the colour—so many anthropomorphic renderings of concepts, aspects and attitudes, as well as photographs of actual lamas, past or present, together with altars hung with silks, decorated with plastic flowers and bearing their offerings of sweets, peanuts and biscuits—finally creates visual and mental rejection, in what is, clearly, my very protestant being! In vain I look for some unity of style which conveys aesthetic and theological harmony. However, I suppose this is unreasonable because Buddhism cannot have a theology, only a philosophy—a philosophy which certainly appears to have more aesthetic harmony in other schools of Buddhism I have encountered than in this one. However, just reading, even more than brief tourist encounters, can be extremely deceptive. That is why, while I struggle with my reactions, I am glad to be doing so earthed in this place.

Bearing in mind my comparison with medieval Europe I was much happier with the small cave *gompa* than this big one. There was a great sense of holiness in that whitewashed cave with its single Buddha figure and limited adornments, but meditating there when we first arrived I was joined by Alison and quickly sensed that this was a special place for her where she needed to be on her own. I have not felt it appropriate to ask her when she uses it because if she thought I was staying away on her account she might be hurt; I also guess that she is up there on many other occasions, polishing the brass with the polish I bought her from Sainsbury's and cleaning the butter-lamps. Alison's peaceful possession of this holy place has now been disrupted by the arrival of a small tense Spanish nun. Having left some clothes there during a previous visit, the Spanish nun has staked a claim to the loft above Alison's potato store, which is where Alison spent her previous retreat. From there the Spanish nun commands a view over the courtyard of the cave *gompa* and exerts her pressure to be the dominant guardian of the cave. Alison is having a bad time and reports, under her breath, that she has even been locked out sometimes and that the Sainsbury's metal polish has been taken over. This is the place where Lama Zopa Rinpoche will live when he comes here for Nyung Na, so no wonder they see each other as rivals. Alison is trying to see the humour of it but the Spanish nun does not have a humorous temperament. I can see she finds it difficult to accept me. I do understand the pull of this exceptional place on both of them, and how I can represent quite an alien presence.

In the main *gompa*, stillness flowed back as Amala withdrew and I closed my eyes to draw myself down into my own stillness, undisturbed by the sights around me and the thoughts to which they gave rise. Before I got up to go across the courtyard to the kitchen for my meal, I bowed my head to the floor as I would have done in a mosque. Immediately I was transported in my mind's eye to the harmonious proportions of the mosques and madrassahs of Samarkand and Bukhara and thought of Tamerlane leaving them to take his great journey across the northern slopes of these mountains to China. I also thought of bowing in the same way among the women in the Al-Aksa mosque on the Temple mount in Jerusalem. This building, which during the western Christians' occupation of Jerusalem in the early years of the twelfth century had been rebuilt by one of the orders of Christian knights, has proportions and harmony which must have spoken in some way of God, even to the rebuilders' bitter enemies, or it would not have been left standing on the site of Solomon's temple with its great pillars and Norman arches and used for Muslim worship to this day.

As I sat and ate my potato pancake on the windowsill of my room these thoughts of the Muslim world returned to me and through them I was led to St Francis—a guru so far away in time—on whom I had planned my afternoon meditation. His image was in front of me on the small card in a rather sentimentalized form. His appearance, as he set out with his companion Illuminato at the beginning of the thirteenth century to encounter the Muslim world, must have been more like yesterday's mountain man in his ragged boots than the trim friar of my pious card. He made this journey to Saladin at Damietta at about the time that the Crusader church was being turned into a mosque, after the fall of Jerusalem to Saladin's troops. It is not clear whether anyone at Damietta knew Francis was coming, but he got there, preached peace to the Crusaders besieging the town and eventually got through the enemy lines. He and Illuminato always sang God's praises as they journeyed and were allowed, under escort, into the Sultan's tent because Saladin was curious about this little holy man. At this period the Muslim world was far in advance of Europe in its accumulated knowledge and the Muslim commanders far more tolerant than the Christians. They had a theological discussion and the Sultan gave Francis a small horn which Francis subsequently used to call people to hear his sermons.

Though the prayer which begins "Make me an instrument of your peace" is probably incorrectly attributed to Francis, I prayed it and meditated upon it in the light of what I remembered about this period of his life. It reminded me of how much he would have identified with the poor people here, how much he would have understood their simple piety—be blowed to architectural style and such things as move me! He would have felt completely at home in Anila's kitchen. Indeed I have thought before, when we were eating there with the men who came to mend Amala's big prayerwheel, how alike this must have been to sitting round a winter fire in the early days of the friars at the Porziuncula.

The mended big prayerwheel—about three feet high in a case like a small open-sided cupboard—is an important feature of Amala's corner of the large room. Here she sleeps and sits most of the day on a pile of blankets. This large wooden area is at bench height. She nearly always has in her hand her small prayerwheel, which she flicks from side to side to turn it. In addition she can now pull the string which turns the large prayerwheel at the same time, with her other hand. This must be something like saying two rosaries at once, and I am sure it earns her much merit. Anyway I do hope so, for as I have got to know her better I really appreciate her toothless smile as I bow on my way past her open door each morning. In preparation for Nyung Na she also has had her head shaved. On it she wears a red cloth hood; below that, with great delight, her glasses. For many years she had cataract and was nearly blind. The doctors at the Hillary hospital at Khunde decided eighteen months ago that they could operate. So Amala was carried in a litter to Namche and then north to Khunde and returned with her sight and the marvellous status symbol of her glasses. As I heard Amala at her prayers in the *gompa* this morning I could not help wondering how consciously, over and above the habit of a lifetime as a nun, so much devotion and prayerful activity for people of her age is undertaken for the accumulation of merit to influence their next incarnation—not that I am belittling this as a motive, for there are many, many more foolish and selfish ways that old ladies spend their time in the West. This morning Alison rubbed her back, which has been aching from an old injury, with arnica ointment. All her skin has the same warm brown glow and is the colour of the soil. She much enjoyed the attention.

I finished my time with Francis this evening thinking about the Canticle of the Creatures, especially about "Sister water—humble, precious and clean"—so precious in this place, so enjoyed by me yesterday. Today the weather would be much too cold, so I was fortunate. Water may be humble, always finding the lowest place, but in so doing it transforms the earth. I thought also how Francis loved the very stuff of the earth itself, how he asked to have his clothes removed as he was dying so that he could lie naked in its embrace. Francis is of course, for me, the Christian equivalent of a *bodhisattva*. He adopted all people as his sisters and brothers and his self-emptying charity began when, overcoming his cultural revulsion at such contact with the unclean, he embraced the leper. From this embrace of a sick brother developed his identification with all the poor. His love of Lady Poverty replaced the ideals of courtly love which had been his as a young man. I think he would have understood the final paradox of the *bodhisattva* vow —refusal to enter nirvana so long as "one single blade of grass remains unenlightened". But I feel he might have doubted his personal importance in that process. His life seems full of very sensual images. At the end I think he regretted how harshly he had treated his body—poor "Sister Ass"—and asked her forgiveness. I thought about his love for all wild creatures, how he used them to flesh out stories to encourage people's understanding and lessen their fear. Though all sentient beings are to be the object of Buddhist compassion, there is none of the personal warmth of Francis that I can discover; and yet Norbu's treatment of the raven was a delightful act which Francis would have applauded. Francis was often heard repeating his mantra—"My Lord and my God"—during his night devotions. I think trying to understand the *bodhisattva* concept in this way, through Francis, is going to be a help. It explains so many different figures which are venerated in this form of Buddhism, so many streams and traditions coming from many sources, sources flowing into the lives of so many awakened beings, who, having transcended their *karma*, remain concerned for all beings still involved in the sufferings of life. This *bodhisattva* compassion colours the way all Sherpas think and feel.

Chapter 18

The lady with the leg

For the last two days a great drama has been playing out here between local and Western medicine. During Sunday, among other local visitors, arrived a young woman friend of Anila's, a widow with four children. She had a wound in her leg from a dog bite which had become septic because she had not been able to clean it properly or rest it. It was swollen and giving her a lot of pain, so she was invited to stay the night. On Monday her leg was worse. She sat in misery by the kitchen fire and Alison offered to look at the wound in case she had some Western medicament in her store with which to treat it. At first Alison simply gave her some painkiller and suggested more rest, but as the condition deteriorated it became a great subject of conversation. The Spanish nun began to take a hand also, passing some hot iron over the leg with certain *puja*s. By the afternoon, when Merry arrived to do some more work on the roof further consultations were held, for the Spanish nun's ministrations had caused some suppurating. Alison and Merry, in spite of themselves, became the representatives of the Western way. Having discovered that the lady had a high temperature Alison applied some antibiotic powder to the wound. She also, in consultation with Anila and Norbu, sent a message down to the hospital in Khunde to ask for advice and the visit of a doctor. (Though all this takes some time, there always seem to be young boys who can be reached to act as runners on these occasions.)

In the meantime Anila, thinking, I suppose, that Western medicine had become the agreed treatment, went to her store of pills and potions left by Western *dharma* students and proceeded in a somewhat haphazard way to administer these also to the hapless woman! By yesterday the leg was a bit less inflamed, so Alison was relieved by this and also by the Khunde doctors who had promised a visit. However, the patient now seemed unable to rouse herself, was deeply depressed and lay all day in a heap on the bench by Amala. By the evening this continued condition led to a local Sherpa consultation at which all agreed: Western treatment was banned and Norbu was hiking it over to the blind lama for *mo*-throwing and more advice. The advice was "Stop all Western medicine and rub the leg with butter," which he had blessed and provided. Alison added, as she told me this part of the story, "Everyone agreed, though, that as it was bound to be stale and would have been in the lama's cave a long while, that it should be applied only around the edge of the wound"! Mantras and prescribed *puja* were also to be said. Today the hospital doctor may arrive.

This morning the woman looks quite perky, having of course recovered from the lethargy and depression induced by the overdosing with various painkilling drugs as well as antibiotics. Alison tells me she even added some codeine before she was aware of Anila's ministrations! It interested me that no local herb, poultice or antiseptic concoction of any kind seemed available in Sherpa medicine for this kind of septicaemia. I cannot help thinking that these skills must have been there in the past but have already been lost. It was only when a mental condition became evident that the Buddhist approach took over and in spite of the doctrine of *karma*, which you would have thought would encourage the development of proven cures other than blessed butter, the medical and physical was overridden by the psychic and spiritual—so much the mirror-image of the Western approach. In the Tibetan tradition there must be some Chinese influence also, but there the aim would be balance. However, some ceremonies are to be performed tomorrow to do with *lung*—the Tibetan for wind or emotions—which may involve this redressing of balance, as it would be in Chinese medicine. The ceremonies must be paid for and done by a monk, so Norbu will preside. The psychological healing must precede the physical.

Alison thinks the wound needs opening and draining, so she hopes the hospital doctor will come.

These Sherpa people are in the classic cross-cultural bind of a poor remote group of people peripheral to the pressures of a once-dominant colonial culture with weakening roots of their own. Presumably, in the Tibetan tradition before the invasion, such people would have been provided by their lamas with help of a strongly rooted kind at all levels which would have been trusted, as the help provided by a medieval monastery would have been trusted. The Sherpas, reintroduced to Tibetan Buddhism in the seventeenth century from the north—it having passed them in the opposite direction en route for Tibet from India in the eighth century—must have been, in their individualistic way in the time between, reverting to B'on and absorbing much from Hinduism. Now, of all the northern Nepalese peoples, they have probably gained more from, and been more influenced by, Western ideas than is realized. I feel that a lot of their adherence to Buddhism is only from convention, with deeper layers of superstition underneath and a questioning scepticism nearer the surface. The blind lama reports that they consult him primarily about buying a field or quarrelling with their wives (not unlike much spiritual direction and counselling in the West!) while he feels he has a spiritual wisdom to offer them; perhaps they simply expect him to throw his *mos*, so he meets their expectations. The numbers of lamas still coming across the border from Tibet and setting up *gompa*s in Nepal may be reaching more Western students than local Sherpas. I shall be interested to see how many local people, especially young people, come to the Nyung Na ceremonies.

As I write this I am sitting in glorious sunshine on my rock behind the *gompa*, while my sleeping-bag gets a rare airing. The old lady has started her midday circumambulations, the beads of her *malla* passing through her fingers as she mumbles her mantra. The white tip of Khumbila to the east is sticking up above a collar of cloud which leaves the Kyajo Drangka valley, lying between us, in deep gloom. South, this flat-bottomed layer of cumulus is also suspended over the Bhute Kosi, at about my level. Above it is a vivid blue sky. This afternoon I might make the ridge beyond the eastern *stupa* for the first time and look up to the glacier of the Kyajo Drangka; but time seems slower in the mountains and I am in no hurry to set out. When I do I am accompanied by the tinkling bell-like sound of the snowfinches.

On my way, as I looked down on Mende, I saw a great lammergeier suspended in the air above the tiny, sunny walled fields. It never stirred a feather, its golden head never turned to either side from the centre of its wide-stretched black wings. As its whole body, held on a rising thermal, inclined away from me, the sun caught its golden breast. Its entire form might have been cut from some rigid material, so without a shadow of movement was its splendid silhouette. Curving into the wind it flattened out again, all in one plane, seemingly totally weightless, totally still, totally silent. Then with no further movement than a great majestic sweep it disappeared into the west. I held my breath. Perhaps this is the bird I had seen on the heights above me several days ago.

I made it to the ridge—I think the highest I have yet climbed: 6,000 metres? The western slopes of Khumbila were only partially veiled in cloud. Immediately opposite me, across the narrow glacier bed the steep shoulder of the mountain was caught by the afternoon sun which highlighted the wet surfaces of the slabs of grey and green rock. Up to my left, as I negotiated the far side of the steep ridge, was the bowl out of which the glacier, now a ribbon of water, flows, still with some patches of ice from the winter at its sides. Coming down the face of this curved, stony dale, from higher sources among the snows, were several steely-blue waterfalls which merged beyond the glacier bed to form the infant Kyajo Drangka stream, which tumbles over white stones and rocks to join the Bhute Kosi just below our crossing point on the way up, by the stout wooden bridge at Phare village. The only habitation between the glacier and the bridge is the impoverished-looking grey stone farm I can look down on from the eastern *stupa*. I took some photos up to the glacier source and then descended slowly back to the *stupa* and sat there in the sunshine eating raisins.

Before seeing the lammergeier and starting my ascent of the ridge, I had been taking photos of the beautiful shy blood-pheasants. While stalking them with my camera I was myself pursued by Bliss and Void. The two *gompa* ravens always keep an eye on what I am up to in this area, as it is probably their territory. I had with me some reject bread with which I hoped to interest the choughs and keep them close enough to snap them also. I threw some to the pink-tied raven and as he flew close to get it I looked up and noticed the figure of a man on the mountain slope above the *gompa*. Taking my binoculars I realized that it was Mike, the Australian staying in the top hermitage. He had disturbed a small musk deer which I could see with my glasses, but which he could not. It was hiding from him behind a scruffy fir. It remained perfectly still for about fifteen minutes before moving off slowly to a greater height. These little deer with their curved front fangs are now protected, having been ruthlessly hunted for so long for their musk glands that they were nearly extinct.

It is now an exceptionally warm and beautiful evening, but already mist is gathering around us and I can sense that it is going to be a cold night like last night. When I had been down to the kitchen and had my hot-water bottle filled by Anila I climbed into my sleeping-bag, and instead of using the time before Alison or Drolkar brought my supper with a kind of recollection, or holding before God, of all my far-flung family and their concerns, as I usually do, I began humming the Taizé chant, "*Ubi caritas.*" After a bit of controlled breathing I managed to make it echo through the empty building. I felt the Buddha of Compassion below me would not object to "Where there is compassion, there is God"—but I did wish I had others to sing it with. The literal emptiness of the two top floors of the *gompa* at night prompted more thoughts on emptiness and solitude. We so often fill this sense of emptiness with needless action to keep at bay our fear of being a "non"-person. Letting go of this person we cling to allows space for things to happen in the psyche. I personally need to allow the psyche to grow in peace towards a greater awareness and creativity, without much assorted clutter from the past. This silence and solitude are marvellous for this letting-go. There is a kind of appropriateness here, a kind of balm in the air. As I fit myself gradually into this place and warm increasingly to its characters they also become increasingly important for me. I value them for the way they are because of, as well as in spite of, our differences. As I cease to judge them by my standards I feel warmer and more positive about myself, discerning the other side of so much of my ordinary activity, the not entirely negative side of needing to be needed. My primary commitments are commitments to people. I so often encourage others to let go of some of these commitments to allow more space for themselves. I must remember this for myself also on my return—balancing it with having a full diary, not for its own sake or to keep emptiness at bay, but to make time and space available for others, to be there for them in their emptiness or loneliness. A form of *caritas?*

Chapter 19

A web of compassion

Thursday 31 May

My Love's birthday. He would be 76. This time ten years ago we spent a very ordinary quiet day at the cottage, having been to Glyndebourne two days before in the BBC box, as a treat. I do not remember what we heard, but I do remember that Marlie, Barbara and Timbo joined us for the weekend.

I use a capital L and claim him as my Love because he is the person with whom I developed the most compassionate form of living I know. We misuse this English word—*love*—so much, reducing it to lust, to possessiveness, to sentimentality and to a trivial emotion to be manipulated by greed. I come back to the Buddha of Compassion: a compassionate love which does not deny eros—the physical attraction, the mysterious chemistry, the sheer givenness of a fulfilling physical relationship—without which a lifelong bond would be absurd. But this compassionate love lives at every level, both with and for the other person, alongside, forgiving and holding, in all circumstances. This kind of loving, through many trials and tragedies, through mistakes and misunderstandings and much plain bloody-mindedness, we grew into together. It was, and still is, a central experience of my whole life. From it our love for our children and grandchildren grew, and I think they would acknowledge that it still permeates the relationships between them and within our family web. The experience of it also permeates for me the relationships in all the other overlapping webs of my life.

I do not use the word *web* as something constraining or binding, but as a fragile but carefully woven support system, woven from the many strands of my life. Sometimes it can be held around me as a warm and protective cloak. At other times it may be heavy with the pain and distress of family and friends. Only at rare moments in my life have I experienced this web as others so often find it—as a kind of trap. For us both, the background to this owed much to the fact that we were supportingly loved as children. Thus compassionate loving extends over time, and at many levels of our relationships can undergird the sense of warm acceptance, of humour and of being available as a resource for those whose experience has been less fortunate.

This brings me close to that other word: *charity*. In recent times charity has grown to mean giving without involvement, without love. Charity is reduced to giving in response to begging, to manipulation, to demand. But even such giving can receive back more than it gave and often more than we are prepared to acknowledge. Thus compassion, in unexpected ways, moves round all kinds of charity. For this English word comes directly from *caritas*—"*Ubi caritas, Deus ibi est*"—where there is charity or compassion God is there. I have just read 1 Corinthians 13, in my King James Bible, using *compassionate love* instead of the seventeenth-century word *charity*. "Compassionate love beareth all things, believeth all things, hopeth all things ..."

The drama of the lady-with-the-leg (as I now call her, for I cannot remember her Sherpa name) took an unexpected turn late yesterday evening. The young Canadian doctor from Khunde hospital set out—on foot, as this is the only possible way—to come to see her. When he got as far as Mende in the late afternoon, he asked the people working in the fields where the woman with the bad leg was, and was informed (Anila says) by a mischief-maker, that it was a Thame woman and that she had gone home. The poor man then walked on to Thame—about four miles —and encountered the woman's family, to be told she was still here. So back he came, arriving as it got dark. Six hours walking to treat one patient! He and Alison talked the case over and by candlelight cut the leg open to allow it to drain. He gave her a big shot of antibiotics, a course of pills for a week and left Alison plenty of dressings for the next few days. He then fell into a sleeping-bag in the room next to mine. I heard him get up at about five o'clock in the morning to walk back to Khunde. Khunde hospital always used to be staffed by New Zealanders, as it was built and financed by the Hillary Trust, but now this young Canadian and his wife, also a doctor, run it with ancillary help from Sherpas. This young couple, Ian and Cathy, enjoy working in out-of-the way places and have already been in Africa. They told Alison that it was rare in the Third World to find a hospital as well funded as Khunde is, where they can afford to pay for two doctors.

He and Alison discussed the role of lamas in the Sherpa health culture. He said that they were excellent, clear-headed and helpful in psychological conditions, but needed to accept the limits of their understanding of physical medicine. Recently, apparently, when a young girl was ill, the lama consulted by her parents ordered two days of *puja* before doing anything else. She had meningitis and by the time Ian got to her it was too late. Another young girl has also died of meningitis this year and in the hospital area seven people have died of altitude sickness —five of them Japanese. He said the Japanese were obsessed with conquering mountain peaks and experimenting with new forms of equipment, but they omitted to take into account the limitations of the human body and tended to push themselves too hard. One other victim was a Sherpa employed by the Japanese, who was expected to go up to the Everest base camp, take photographs and return, in a time which was unreasonably short even for a Sherpa. Anxious to fulfil his contract and get the money the young man pushed himself, with fatal results. The last casualty was a Mexican man of 64 who was with a party of younger people, and again tried too hard to keep up. Older people apparently generally prove less susceptible to altitude sickness. The hospital has a portable form of decompression apparatus, but getting down from the high places on foot always includes some climbing back again to higher altitudes, at which points the patient can go into a coma.

I have just been in the kitchen drinking tea with the lady-with-the-leg and her young daughter, who is now also in residence. All is smiles and relief. It looks as if my retreat discipline is slipping! Is this a soft option or can it really be justified to take advantage of a unique and never-to-be-repeated chance to share the life of this small community? I think of Bernard doing his Zen meditation in the small garden hut at

Tao Fong Shan, and of the strict prescriptions of length of time and subjects for meditation, of hermits here. I think also of my own past strict commitments, like the Friday three hours of silent prayer in Westminster Abbey, which I did for nearly ten years. All these times, subjects for meditation and other disciplines, are only tools we use to move beyond them. I retain the image of the pane of glass which emerged from a conversation with Ann Bancroft and Aelred Graham at a Zen–Christian weekend in Stepney. We were talking about the graceful branch of a plane tree outside my bedroom window in London, which formed the focus of my morning meditations at that time, and how to move beyond the object–subject duality. To move beyond duality and the sense of separateness you need to remove "the pane of glass". This has been my symbol since then of becoming part of all that is around me. There is also a kind of outward looking that informs the inward seeing, until "the eyes of my eyes are open, the ears of my ears awake". This is the discipline I am committed to. It can be practised in solitude or company, in noise and chaos as well as in silence.

Today I offered my services as a painter of the *gompa* windows. As Merry is not expected to come over this afternoon the team preparing for Nyung Na will be one short. Alison seemed a bit surprised by my offer as I am in retreat. Not being a Buddhist under obedience to a lama it must indeed appear that I am making my retreat rules as I go along. But beyond the short conversations in pidgin which keep me related to the Sherpa community, I do speak as little as possible and listen as much as I can. There is no reason to chat while I paint, but it will continue to demonstrate that I want to help. I reassured Alison that there was a long tradition of manual labour in Christian retreats. The others were working outside the building and I was painting the windows from the inside, each narrow moulding being picked out in a different bright colour— blue, red, yellow or green. The windows were open to the sun and it was a beautiful morning. As the prayer flag in the courtyard fluttered on its tall pole, "*labore est orare*" I thought to myself and realized what a stable, centred Benedictine time this stay in Lawudo had turned out to be—a new setting for the Benedictine rules of stability and openness to change. I remembered the Zen story of the Ch'an Buddhist patriarch of China: Is it the flag that moves? Is it the wind? Neither, it is your mind.

Behind me the four Buddha statues on the altar look quite unmoved with
their bright painted eyes. I am pleased to be here with them because I am
just beginning to learn about the smaller green figure on Chenrezi's left.
It is his consort Tara, a female figure of wisdom and compassion, who
was absorbed from various Yoga cults into the tantric tradition—green
Tara, the *bodhisattva* of female energies. As Buddhism moved east
Avolokita/Chenrezi took on more and more female attributes until in
some parts of China he and Tara became one. I relate better to her in
her "greenness" than to Chenrezi, with all his arms and eye-filled hands.
I relate also to this tantric injunction which I have just read: "See all
beings as Buddhas, hear all sounds as Mantra and perceive all places to
be Nirvana." The simplicity of this offsets for me what otherwise
appears complicated and confusing in the Buddhism which surrounds
me.

I ate one of my two remaining crunchy bars after my lunch of
steamed dumplings today, to celebrate Tim's birthday. I would much
rather it had been fruit, which I truly miss after so many weeks. I shall
have the other crunchy bar on Sunday, which is Pentecost. Tim's mother
had a bad time when he was born, probably because she was terribly
afraid of pain. He was small and weak and known as "the puny
pentecostal babe". This fear, this real inability to handle pain and come
to terms of some kind with it, stayed with my mother-in-law all her life.
It drove her, in her early sixties, to have all her perfectly good teeth out
because she could not face visits to the dentist. Also she had only one
more child, sixteen years after Tim, when she found a doctor who
promised he could make her labour pain-free. In so many other ways she
was a very courageous woman. She had beautiful red hair, which when
she was a young girl was dressed in the fashion of the beginning of the
century, on the top of the head. She looked like one of Rossetti's
romantic red-haired beauties. I believe that people with this pigmentation
have a much lower pain threshold than people with a different colouring.
She was a formidably militant atheist and never allowed herself to
discover, in the universe or in any personal relationship, that degree of
love which casts out fear.

I went after dark this evening to fetch a shirt which I had left tied to
a tree on my way to the eastern *stupa* yesterday. I looked up as I was

pulling it free and there, apparently suspended from heaven, was the summit of Kwangde. It looked like a triangle of mottled, beaten copper hanging above the dark cloudbank behind which the other peaks had already been overtaken by night. Its craggy height must mean that it catches the very last rays of the setting sun on this western face of its summit.

Chapter 20

Open mind

Overslept. Nice sunny day. I had a really good wash in my room and then took my clothes and my water-can to the pipe. Having given my clothes a good wash there, I filled my plastic container and returned to hang the clothes out to dry on my usual tree by the *gompa* rock. Then establishing myself on the rock with rug and books I fetched my potato-noodle lunch from Anila and sat eating it in the sun.

I have been reading the transcript of a lecture given in Germany by Lama Yeshe, who was Lama Zopa's teacher—on the gradual path to enlightenment. He began with the three principles: *bodhicitta* (open-mindedness), renunciation and *shunyata* (wisdom). In relation to the first I like his phrase "the mind open like space ... allowing all living beings." Then he complains of the dualistic mind. "Narrow," he says. "To be happy we have to eliminate that one." When Westerners think of such elimination they suppose that thought—thinking *about* things, the most used part of *our* mind—is to be suppressed when someone from the East speaks. But it is this subject–object dualism which is rejected. Plenty of thought goes on here, particularly at the practical level. I think it more a question of giving equal value to thought and intuition. The latter will prove its importance when acknowledged and appreciated. Then some more profound way of experiencing the world and making choices emerges from this weaving together. One strong thread from two strands united proves a more reliable tool of action, understanding and compassion than a single approach.

I remember this impressive, humorous man when he came to
London in the 1970s. At a meeting in the old Kensington town hall he
joked with all his questioners and gave me my first taste of Tibetan
Buddhism. In the sedate Victorian council chamber hung incongruously
with coloured streamers, he was accompanied by Lama Zopa, at that
time a young man who stood unsmiling and solemn beside him. I
remember how Lama Yeshe, in reply to one questioner, spoke about his
great respect for Jesus.

When I read how Lama Yeshe talks about the categories and
distinctions of Western thought leading to dualism, I reflect how close
Lama Yeshe's descriptions of this attitude are to the descriptions and
categorizing of all the interior psychological states and conditions listed
in tantric writings. It is as if wisdom, compassion and unselfishness or
indeed lust, hatred and envy had to be categorized in order to be
attached to a specific *bodhisattva* or particular representation of evil; then
a statue is made and put "out there". This surely creates a distinct
dualism, because the student then has to be reminded that these are only
representations of the deities, and the deities themselves are only aspects
of our own nature. This seems to me to be a kind of circular double-
bind. Meditate on these "aspects" portrayed by the statues externally
before you, identify with the aspects which lead to wholeness and
compassion and reject those which lead to dualism, and detach yourself
from the representations of the concepts, because all external problems
are really caused within you. Do so many statues really help? Surely the
"Buddha mind" is something simpler and more direct than all that. It
drives me back to Zen as well as to the Tao. In meditation "I" and the
flower can be one. The clutter of my mind is what erects a pane of glass
between us. Dissolve the clutter, empty my mind—"beginner's mind" to
"open mind"—to dissolve the dualism, and go with the flow. I wish it
was as easy as that!

I must stop my own kind of double-bind—letting all this judging,
categorizing and feeble attempts at understanding—come between me
and any true hope of open-mindedness. My mind needs to be open to
my own spiritual poverty. I wish I had some Eckhart with me, but that
too is like reaching for another prop. Somewhere he talks about the birth
which wells up from within and reverses the whole process of knowing.

He also talks about stripping away all that diverts or fragments. The kind of thinking I have recently been allowing myself to move into certainly does that. Enough. Stay within the silence of a peaceful open mind.

Last night, just as I was about to go to sleep, it came into my head —the second half of the collect for Quinquagesima: "... Therefore Almighty God instil into our hearts that inestimable gift of charity, without which whosoever liveth is accounted dead before Thee." I did not search for it; it came to me complete. It has something to do with the subject of my meditations yesterday. Eckhart said, "When I am in the flow"—and by "the flow" he meant engaged in the ordinary affairs of life with an open mind—"all things speak to me of God because of the stillness in the ground of my soul." The more I have been able to let myself go into the flow of this place and in many ways the less I have struggled—as this morning—with the questions that this form of Buddhism raises for me and the more I enjoy feeling at home with these people and the surrounding natural splendour, the greater grows the stillness in the ground of my soul. From this stillness, openness and acceptance within "the flow" came this restoration of memory.

I had a very flowing conversation yesterday with an ex-monk of Lama Zopa's, who is a new visitor to Lawudo, now inhabiting one of the bottom cells. I met him with his puppy on my walk to the eastern *stupa*: a tousled Australian in hippy gear. We talked sitting on the *stupa* ledge high above the Mende fields and he told me about his unconventional life and his daughter called Tara in Australia. When I told him I was a Christian he said, "Good, we need the diversity." This helped me to make a shift which connected our conversation with a sense of acceptance by the "Western" visitors as well as the Sherpa family, so that both areas of relatedness could flow into my inner stillness. Being accepted at both these levels should help me to let go of that still-present niggle that there must still be something for me to try to understand. It is as if I was in some way disappointed with my own intellectual inability to grasp the particular "point" of this kind of Buddhism. Why should there be a point? It has grown from its own roots and its own history and just *is*. This has helped me to realize that I need not worry to understand any more. We need the diversity. I have my own roots and my own path which leads me, if not to an enlightened, at least to a moderately open mind. It is this path also which has led me into any such spiritual maturity as I have and which finds its acceptance in all that I share with these people. So ... questing mind be still, enlightened mind be open. "See all beings as Buddha, hear all sounds as Mantra, and perceive all places to be Nirvana."

Other children of the lady-with-the-leg are here today including a small boy called Ano, whose wary look when he first saw me crumpled into an engaging gap-toothed smile. His Mum is getting better and should be home soon. She is constantly at work in the kitchen, while Anila feeds them all. The painting of the *gompa* continues. I did not help today as there were not enough narrow brushes to go round for the window work. Some Germans appeared after lunch on a one-day trek from Namche. Alison gave them the tour and directions for reaching the Cherok Lama. One of them had been to Gokyo two days ago and said how beautiful the lake had been in the bright sunshine. I rather regret not having the energy to make a four- or five-day trip up there when my retreat and Nyung Na are over. Well, so be it. Probably loss of stability and flow would result. On the surface these two words seem contradictory. In fact, at the spiritual level, they are complementary.

This morning on my way back from the water pipe there was a sudden flash of vivid orange. It was the spread tail of the tiny yellow-bellied fantail in among the juniper catching flies. Later on I saw the large peacock-like monal, which the Sherpas call *danphe*, having a wonderful time at the end of the top potato patch. At first I thought it was having a dust bath, but as it kept scratching the soil to make a deeper and deeper hole I realized that it was digging for potatoes to eat. I clapped my hands to scare it off. When I told Anila about this greedy *danphe* when getting my thermos flask filled up this evening, she already knew and said she might put some sticks over the end of the plot. Otherwise she was quite prepared to share the results of her hard labour with any needy creature.

• Anila with her 100-year-old pestle and mortar

overleaf: • Norbu with yak • Anu on steps • The little girl from Mende with her puppy
• Amala with her prayerwheel, on the balcony above the stable

Kwangde (20,300ft)

Tang Kampoche (21,326ft)   *Trashi Labtsa*

Chapter 21

Interconnections

"Go about the world acknowledging that which is of God in everyman," wrote George Fox. I have just thought of this and it seems to me to be the perfect English translation of the greeting *Namaste*—often translated into English as "I recognize the divine in you." Naturally a lot of the time this is said without thought, like most greetings. This particularly applies to "How do you do?" because we seldom wait for a reply or would care if there was one. But what is acknowledged in this greeting? Is there a transcendent element in Buddhism—so that it is inaccurate to think it is only a philosophy? Our Western passion for defining ever smaller parts and thus breaking up the whole has been taken into our understanding of God: thus we see the divine in everyman as an aspect of God's Spirit—perhaps a fragmented aspect within each of us—but the Spirit is one.

I found myself dwelling on all the symbols of the Spirit which are part of my mental furniture. The tongues of flame which appeared above Jesus' friends at Pentecost. Flame which consumes but also gives light. The symbol of light—the Spirit within, which enlightens everyone;

• *Alison pounding incense by the front of the kitchen*

previous page:
• *Early-morning panorama from my window on a clear day, looking southwest*

the light of every new morning, the light of truth which nourishes the enlightened mind. The symbol of the dove. That bird bringing the assurance of God's peace to Noah; the connecting life-giving Spirit which hovers between Mary and the angel when she accepts her creative role at the Annunciation. The peace of this Spirit is not an easy peace, but challenges us always to make the connections and to be creative with our own chaos and the chaos of our own times. This aspect of the Trinitarian God undermines dualism, is *the* interconnector, the Spirit that comes and goes but remains the indwelling God, the God within. "Let God be God in you," wrote Eckhart. This interior but interconnecting Spirit is praying in us before we have found words, is silent in us before we have found stillness, and in this Spirit we recognize all which is of God in others. Is this sort of thing as complicated as I find the pantheon of Buddha-aspects, archetypal deities and *bodhisattva*s?

The inter-connectedness, the relatedness, of the three persons of the Trinity is what is so moving in the Rublev ikon—the next card in my window shrine. These persons are depicted as the three men who appeared to Abraham in the heat of the day, outside his tent at Mamre. They are not particularly masculine figures: their hair is long, their tunics and upper garments soft and flowing in muted tones of brown, blue and green. They have large yellow wings which are almost part of the rocky yellow and green landscape behind them. They sit round a table, which is also an altar and which could also be a tomb. They seem deeply involved with one another and all look at a chalice which is on the table. A great deal has been written about this ikon of the three angels sent to Abraham, whom he received as special messengers from God and who prophesied that Sarah, his barren wife, would bear a son in her old age. I wonder why Rublev chose to portray them as the three persons of the Trinity. I have no idea whether the connection had been made before. The angels are certainly closely involved with one another, perhaps concerned about the sacrifice of Christ, as they turn towards the chalice on the table. This must be linked with the horror of the demand on Abraham to sacrifice that promised son Isaac, yet to be born. It seems to be about love and sacrifice being connected; about loving relationships. The greens and blues of the beautifully draped clothes are echoed in the tree on the right behind the figures and the more distant sky above them. This conveys the inclusion of the natural world in their concern. The deep yellow of the messengers' wings and the soft yellows and browns of the surrounding rocks give an impression of great gentleness and calm but also of a movement spiralling into the centre where the cup stands. The whole scene is calm and gentle yet mysterious, suggesting the elusive way another dimension can break through into the normal day. This slippery quality, this many-faceted nature of reality, is something I should allow into my musings about Buddhism. I think it would help me to a better understanding of Buddha-aspects and manifestations, deities and *bodhisattva*s. For surely Buddhism is not just a philosophy to be intellectually grappled with—it is lived at many levels. I must allow that there is a mystical Buddha just as there is a mystical Christ. I was so looking forward to seeing the original of the Rublev ikon on my only visit to Moscow, but the gallery was closed.

It has been a strange day in many ways. I set out this morning to visit Merry's cave, did not keep to the right path round the mountain and ended up among a group of unknown buildings. Some were ruined, some clearly occupied, with prayer flags and vegetable plots. There was a lovely spring of water and some of the biggest and most beautiful trees I have seen up here. But in spite of my calls, which echoed back from the rocks, there was no reply and no one about. I clambered up and down among the shrubs and clumps of spurge and primula. Because I had been anticipating meeting people, if not Merry then probably the blind lama's daughter and grandson, I found the emptiness in this unexpected place quite eerie. However it was only a passing feeling and I sat still on a rock in the sun for some time listening to the sound of the clear spring water splashing over the stones and imagining living in this hollow of tall pines. Then I had to retrace my steps which, to my surprise, led me onto my familiar path to the water pipe.

I lingered where the stream crosses the boggy area which forms what I think of as my miniature rock-garden open to the sky and the winds. What a contrast to the precious haven of my London garden where my solitude or quietness is guarded by the walls covered in creepers and the two enormous plane trees sheltering the space beneath and continually showering it with leaves, bobbles of seeds, opened calyxes or bark. In spite of the work these trees generate at every season, this place is still my oasis of peace, where in an unexpected silence for the centre of the city I can do my *t'ai chi* in the early morning, eat my meals in the shade, get a tan in the sun and write and read in peace. It is the place where I potter with plants and satisfy my need to be nurturing something and to be in touch with the soil. Above me usually croak the crows, my two familiars of 40 years, building their untidy nests and unfortunately preying on the baby bluetits, sparrows and even blackbirds, which nest in my shrubs and wall-creeping plants. In spring and autumn skeins of geese fly over on their way between the canal and the Serpentine, and in stormy weather gulls circle round screeching or sit in a line on the ridge of the church roof opposite.

During the afternoon I finished painting the inside of the courtyard gates green, while Alison was painting complicated lotus designs on the outside in different colours. While we were doing this, the doctors from Khunde, Ian and his wife Catharine, turned up to see the lady-with-the-leg and to stay the night on their way down to the Sherpa dancing festival of Mani Rimdu at Thami tomorrow. I would like to have joined them as this festival is a great annual Sherpa occasion, but I don't think I can face competing for accommodation of a pretty basic kind with an influx of locals and visitors. Ian and Catharine were interesting about their work. They have been at Khunde a year and have another year to go. Catharine is anxious to train and build up the confidence of auxiliary medics—all women—in the surrounding villages. She feels these local people should be the first point of reference for anyone needing medical attention. Their training should enable them to deal with many cases which now fill the surgeries at the hospital. When these local auxiliaries are bypassed or ignored, the system of aftercare is also weakened. They had some hair-raising case histories to tell, particularly about women in labour. There is a taboo about women speaking about gynaecological difficulties and if they need help, they get to the hospital only in advanced stages of labour with all sorts of complications.

One of the most common ordinary complaints in this area, they said, is stomach ulcers because of the indigestible spiced food and because of drinking *chang* and *rakshi*. Also there is bronchitis among women because they sit for so long over their cooking stoves breathing in the smoke. But few people develop many complaints common in the West. There are, however, two illnesses unique to Sherpas, the names of which I cannot remember. One is a type of depression where the patient —usually a woman—grows fat but feels light and out of control and often shuts herself up in her house and will not see anyone. The other is a form of migraine. Both these complaints must be psychosomatic in origin—just the kind of conditions lamas might indeed have the best cures for.

Leaving the painting and the talk I walked down the path past the lower cells. I am, I think, getting more deeply into the inner process of what is happening to me here in spite of keeping up my contacts with the inhabitants and visitors to Lawudo. I am beginning to understand that if I am to work through some of this intellectual questioning alone, my openmindedness must apply to myself. I tend to set myself goals, in answer to this questioning, of some kind of rational understanding and yet the criteria by which I live most of the time is a far more intuitive way of arriving at conclusions. Perhaps I could try some more specific Buddhist meditation practice like imaging a positive *bodhisattva* quality and then taking it into myself. This might free me from the sort of negative spiral I get into when I fail to discover, in myself, the answers to my own questions. However, I still find it difficult to bridge the Buddhist ideal of the "not-self" with the Christian idea of personhood. But I think I was originally drawn to Buddhism because I found the Christian concentration on the person of Jesus a bit unbalanced. I remember taking an interested Muslim friend to a church service. At the end he asked, "Where was God in all that? He was only mentioned as Father." All I could say was that Jesus was the human ikon of God. Through him we knew God in human form. I have always been Theo-centric rather than Christo-centric in my own prayer and meditation, and therefore I perfectly understood his question. I also understand now how I hoped the philosophical framework of Buddhism would help my devotional practice.

Well, part of my devotional practice is to move through the world with all my senses alert, recognizing over and over again that the divine is not outside somewhere, but within all matter. One of the things that first drew me to the writings of Teilhard de Chardin was a sentence from one

of his letters from the trenches in the First World War—I think—in
which he wrote: "Some may wish to worship God as pure spirit, but I, as
an incarnate being, worship him in all the fibres of the world." The
Japanese Christian Kagawa wrote in similar terms of matter as "the
garment of the divine." We go around half-asleep, with our senses dulled
and so see only the garment. Letting go of the layers of convention in
this way of "seeing" is like peeling off the skins of an onion to discover
a more immediate awareness. In my retreats I encourage people to slow
down, starting with being conscious of their breathing and physical
movements, to let go of tensions and preoccupation with goals, and so
to move into this greater awareness that the experience of a deeper
seeing and hearing can be theirs. "The eyes of my eyes are open / the
ears of my ears awake," as the poet e. e. cummings wrote.

Ignatius Loyola's aim for a retreat—"finding God in all things and
all things in God"—is so close to the verse in the *Bhagavad Gita*
describing the seeker who is one with God "seeing himself in the heart
of all beings and all beings in his own heart ... a vision which is ever
one." For Westerners it is so difficult to slow down enough to reach this
different level of awareness because our attention is always moving on to
the next thing. So when I encourage people to move with all their senses
alert into the world around them, I use a Zen saying: "Find some object.
Do not move on to another object. For in this object is the blessing." To
enter into any awareness exercises of this kind, I find it is helpful to have
spent some time relaxing the body and becoming aware of the tensions
held there, listening to the body's needs in the context of Julian of
Norwich's understanding that we are "soul and body enclosed in the
goodness of God." Only when the connections have been made with
God's presence in these ways do I find it possible to move on creatively
to work with people's experience of guilt and suffering. It is good to
learn, every now and again, that in walking beside them for these short,
rather intensive periods of retreat you have in some way been an enabler
of a greater awareness of reality. Perhaps I am recalling and writing this
now in order to tell myself, because I feel the absence of such an enabler,
that awareness and openmindedness will also bring me assurance of God
in all things—a vision which is ever one.

Chapter 22

Searching and fitting in

"*Veni, Sancti Spiritus,*" I hum under my breath to the Taizé tune as I remember from Siegfried Sassoon's poem *Pentecost*, "Spirit that works through silences, remake me," going down rather late to the kitchen for my breakfast of *tsampa*. Merry and Alison are already there explaining to the young doctors the significance of Nyung Na, so I stay and listen. I can tell there is a slight tension for Alison as she hears Merry interpret the coming ritual in a rather detached way. Alison said to me afterwards, "I don't think hearing Merry's negative thoughts is helpful for people." "Well," I said, "she has been involved with this form of Buddhism for a long time. The individual understandings and differences are bound to emerge. You are at an earlier stage." "I think the honeymoon period is coming to an end, though, especially with regard to Zopa Rinpoche," Alison replied. I said nothing, but certainly am doubtful that this is so. However, I could make out a case for her seeing this environment as somewhere she can let go of responsibility, handing personal decisions over to Lama Zopa and forgetting about the stress and burdens of her last London job. The special voice in which she tells stories about him is in the same naive way she told me how encouraging it was to be in a dormitory of young Western devotees, each with only a few inches between their beds, where they had all made little altars and offerings. I could not help envisaging a dormitory of young born-again Christians on a youth mission weekend, with their Jesus-loves-me slogans, or a convent school retreat with other little altars, pictures and rosaries. But eventually this is not enough in any spiritual tradition. The bad experiences which Ian and many Western devotees here have had of Christianity has so much to do with a whole institutional inability to help people move on to a more mature type of spirituality, as well as institutional identification with the conventions of society.

Of course it is encouraging when any groups of young people find some inspiration which helps them to discover ideals in an aggressively material world, but such enthusiasm can still be found in all religions. The really sad thing for me is that very few of these young Westerners have ever given Christianity a real try, simply equating school or parish worship with the totality of the spiritual tradition. Even Alison, though full of enthusiasm at the time of her involvement with Christianity, had very little idea of the depth and variety of this tradition and confused it with the moralizing activism and social convention she encountered in her home parish. For Westerners there is an additional fascination with Tibetan Buddhism of a remote, colourful and alien culture. I saw the whole pull at work with one of my nephews, first of all with the Divine Light Mission and then the Hare Krishna movement, as he sought some spiritual way of life which would free him from a society which he had experienced as very repressive. When you are struggling hard to find your own identity you have to explore further afield than those who feel they fit in with the status quo. I like to think, however, that such young people might also be helped by exploring rather than rejecting Christianity. But there is nothing so counterproductive in these circumstances as official sanction allied with the deadliness of most church services. Another major cause of disaffection is a rejection of the philosophical idea of a God who is presented in these services as remote but controlling and therefore responsible for the mess that the world is in. This is Buddhism's greatest strength: it posits no God "out there" and is concerned with inner development and right action. But if these young devotees had experimented with some of the monastic and mystical traditions of the West which parallel much of Buddhist teaching, they would be in a better position to make a judgement. However, who am I to judge, because I am not making great progress at moving out of the way I think at the moment. Perhaps I never will. It is

an intellectual tool of my culture, which I understand and which
nourishes me at many other levels. It is sad that as Christians we are not
so confident any more in offering our spiritual traditions as alternative
ways into an understanding of the mystery of life, rather than what is
seen as boring religious and social conformity.

Well, I too am at fault. I do not do it even here. I do not say, "But
you are not comparing like with like. You are comparing the personal
attention of a guru to your own spiritual growth, with the *puja* in a local
temple." But I keep quiet because I do not want to offend such
supportive and kind friends. Perhaps that is just a feeble excuse? With
this question in mind I walked down to Alison, who is still painting the
lotus pattern on the courtyard gate, with nothing particular in mind other
than the need to communicate. However, we had a conversation
something like this:

"Today is Whit Sunday."

"Oh, I knew it was Sunday, but not that it was that one," Alison
replied.

"The day of the spirit of 'the light and power of love'," I
continued, half-amused by taking on this role.

"Define love," said Alison, ever really a Westerner.

"Come on, I am not going to do the defining. Perhaps you can
define compassion. For we both know that the word love is about the
most abused in the English language so I can only point to some
synonyms which are appropriate, and compassion would be one of
them."

"His Holiness," Alison said, meaning the Dalai Lama, "defined love
as wanting someone else's happiness."

"Well, what did he mean by happiness? There are many kinds of
happiness also."

I thought again about these two words later. *Com-passion*, meaning
to "suffer-with", is consistent with the Buddhist view that life is
suffering. If life also includes joy and happiness as Christians believe,
then *love*, the word for sharing and sympathy, is bound to be uppermost:
"suffering with" balanced by "enjoying with". It was really quite a
flowing conversation, though it sounds a bit priggish when written
down. It developed in a flowing way too and ended with our singing, as

she painted and I sat on the hillside, some of Alison's favourite hymns in doubtful unison. Merry looked surprised as she passed, carrying water, which we need in great quantities for the Nyung Na crowds.

"It's Whit Sunday," Alison said.

"Oh," said Merry. "I saw it in my diary and wondered what it meant." We explained the origins.

As it was getting late the *gompa* was empty, so I slipped in on my way back to my cell. Sitting there I regretted that I had not had time to read more about Tibetan Buddhism's spirituality and art before I came. I am putting myself in the same position as the young Westerners I complain of. However limited my success I am at least trying to understand the spiritual tradition, but I feel sure my ignorance affects the superficiality of my understanding of the art. Nothing here is likely to be the best of the tradition, but as I sit and look more closely at the little green Tara at the foot of Chenrezi and some of the *thangka*s on the walls I realize that, as with the ikon, their true significance can emerge only with faith. I think I get a bit closer to absorbing the symbolism, however, every time I look at these artefacts in a meditative and uncritical way.

Shadows were filling the valleys as I returned to my cell and it was getting cold, so I went down again to the kitchen and dear Anila filled my hot-water bottle. As I scrambled into my night clothes, putting my anorak on top, and got into my sleeping-bag I suddenly regretted all absence of news from the outside world. I have never had this feeling here before and it took me by surprise. Drolkar's arrival with my Sherpa stew for supper soon dispelled this mood. Perhaps the low was due to hunger. Anyway I know what a valuable experience it is to be here, and a large part of the value is remoteness and escape from perpetual bombardment from the media. My almost greedy desire to understand at a deeper level all that is involved in the Tibetan Buddhist faith and culture around me is an interesting parallel to my persistent pursuit of God. In this pre-monsoon weather, when the mist envelops the mountain, I so often long for it to lift so that I can wander among the bright flowers and birds, all my energy out in my eyes. Seeing is for me the primary, most objective way of knowing. My other senses seem less acute, less focused. Intellectual perception is a kind of inner seeing. This is the understanding I thirst for. Being content with misty intimations within, of the unknowable, unseeable God, without struggling to intellectually objectify them is like sitting in my mountain cell surrounded by the exterior mist as darkness falls and being content just to sit in this silence and darkness.

For Tim, the thought of death was entering into a dazzling, not a misty, darkness. It is an image which goes back to the earliest Christian writers like Origen and comes through in gentler form in George Herbert. Here close to the crags where the eagles sit, co-inhabiting the mist, another powerful image for my own thirst comes to my mind: the soaring bird of prey of St John of the Cross, that rises higher and higher to catch what it desires. Do eagles soar in the mist? In clear weather an eagle's sight gives it control, but in the mist I wonder how its behaviour changes. Here in my cell any sounds are a long way off tonight like the intimations of God's presence in my soul. Abba Moses said, "Go and sit in your cell, and your cell will teach you everything." My soul is clothed in mist in divine darkness as my cell is surrounded by mist in the Nepalese night.

This is the re-making, transforming silence which I came for, however hard it is to express it. "In quietness is my strength"—I hope, and not just the sluggish pulse of increasing age. Otherwise I think I have been writing some rather pompous notes today. This is not what I intended. Perhaps I get more pompous and into my comparative-studies mode when I allow myself to be diverted into conversations with Alison like the one today, which take me away from the silence of acceptance, the silence of mindfulness.

Chapter 23

Painting the gompa

Sunday is the day I allow myself to read the week's entries in this journal. Perhaps I will do it this evening; there is no time at the moment, for I must continue to recount the progress of two interlocking dramas: the lady-with-the-leg and the preparations for Nyung Na. Yesterday evening, when Ian the doctor arrived, the lady-with-the-leg had been in a lot more pain. He discovered that she had another abscess behind the old one, and when he had lanced it, to her horror, he inserted a drainage tube. She is most distressed, for this tube seems like an alien presence in her flesh. Ian and his wife slept here the night, in the room next to mine. They left for Thami, for the beginning of the Mani Rimdu (masked dance) festival, early in the morning. They have taken the weekend off and should return tomorrow for some of the Nyung Na rituals.

All day yesterday frantic preparations for the arrival of Lama Zopa were underway. In the *gompa* painting, cleaning, tidying and flower-arranging were in progress. The last is a great labour because the rhododendrons, which are considered appropriate on such occasions, can be found in flower only at much higher altitudes than ours. Those who climb and pick them then have to find an old tin which does not leak, and which has not been commandeered for some important domestic function, before the flowers can be put in the *gompa*. The Spanish nun is painting small Buddha statues with gold paint and Alison is still working on the main gate. Some of the Mende children have caught the atmosphere of tension and expectation and have come up with their friends and a puppy to see what is going on. Many of them have joined the water-carriers.

This morning all the mountains and valleys were wreathed in cloud and if these conditions continue, as is highly likely, there is no way the Lama's plane is going to arrive on the specially opened Shyangboche airstrip near Namche. So the day, like a piece of loose elastic, has gradually lost its tension and ended at a gentle and relaxed pace. This gives Alison and Norbu plenty of time to complete preparations they had not managed to fit in yesterday. I have taken advantage of this spaciousness to finalize our departure arrangements for Saturday with Alison, as it will be inappropriate for me to talk to her once the Nyung Na rituals begin. I cannot believe that we have reached this point in our stay and already I am experiencing those mixed feelings about saying goodbye to such lovely people and yet being able to think with relief of only three more Sherpa stews, only two more indigestible bean mixtures and, best of all, only about six more nights in my flea-bag!

The relaxed, slack feeling applied in the kitchen as well tonight, and I am waiting for Drolkar, who wants to bring me my supper as usual. I am sitting in my sleeping-bag on my wooden bed in my wooden cell, wondering whether this will be the last evening of this kind of peace and solitude. Certainly things will be quite different if the Lama and his following arrive tomorrow. Opposite me now is the reflection of my trembling candle flame in the window. The shadows of the candle leap up and down on the dark walls and reveal, depending on which way the air moves the flame, my few simple objects ranged round the walls. My big pack, with my clothes in it, remains in shadow at the end of my bed. On the bench under the window, below my simple shrine, are a rug of Norbu's and a few books. Beside the bench my boots and my Raasay stick are leaning together with the brush I made from juniper twigs to sweep the floor. My small day-pack leans against the right-hand wall next to the plastic water bucket and the old enamel soup bowl in which I wash. On the next wall is a small wooden shelf with my toothbrush, thermos, mug and a nearly empty biscuit packet. Across from the shelf to a nail by the door is a piece of string on which hangs my towel. Then comes the door with its wooden latch, which is next to my bed. Not a

room with a lot in it. The light from the candle flame glints on the red
plastic of the bucket and on the thermos on the shelf. I value the
simplicity and stability of the life I have led here exemplified in these few
things, the sense that everything has an appropriate use and that nothing
is superfluous. It is just good to pick up the tin mug and drink from it—
no more, no less. It seems part of the silence which surrounds me. A
silence which is at one with the single flame standing out against the
surrounding dark, a not unfriendly dark, but one in which any sound is
muffled because the darkness is not only the dark of night but also the
darkness of high cloud enclosing the silence of the highest peaks.

Monday 4 June

The elastic began to tighten again this morning. Despite heavy cloud
there were some patches of blue sky and Norbu thought the plane would
come and that between ten and eleven we might see the Lama's party
emerge out of the mist into the Mende fields. Alison, on the other hand,
after a strong *puja* yesterday evening, had decided that he was not going
to come for another week. She overslept, which is unusual, and during
her sleep dreamt of a plane disgorging lots of cars on Mende, like
bombs from a bomber. The lady-with-the-leg is better and moving about
more happily. I have not asked about the drainage tube because it is a
sore point with all the Sherpas. They resent the fact that Ian did not
explain its purpose to her. She has been helping Amala to open the
balcony doors and straighten out the big room. I have never seen it look
so large, light and airy. The painting of the exterior woodwork of the
gompa continues. Revolving around all these preparations are the personal
agendas of those for whom Lama Zopa's arrival is an important event.
The Spanish nun and Alison have a lot of emotional investment in him.
Being chosen or accepted by a teacher involves a two-way personal
commitment and rapport. Alison and the nun, in their small two-
storeyed building, are the only inhabitants of the cave courtyard. Lama
Zopa is the reincarnation of the Lawudo Lama who lived in this cave
and this is his place when he is here. I can understand that proximity
with him is important to them both. The Spanish nun lives in the loft of
the small building at right angles to the cave and Alison lives in the

potato store underneath, which she shares with a few rats.

The high point of their rivalry is the question about who is to take care of the cave. Alison arrived first and began cleaning and tidying, filling the lamps and waterpots and using it as the place for her meditations. It is a much more peaceful place than the large *gompa* and if I had not been conscious of intruding on her, I think I would have found it much easier to meditate in there than in any other place in Lawudo. Anyway when the Spanish nun arrived she began to take over. Maybe her position as a nun, or just her age, gave her precedence. She has a reputation for a fiery temperament. I could tell that Alison was gradually having to give way. Three days ago the tension was such that she would not even be in the same building as the nun and they have been working on quite different painting projects. Yesterday Alison told me that she had been quite dispossessed of the cave and that the Spanish nun was using the brass-cleaner for the lamps that I had provided from Sainsbury's. Rather a different scene from North Kensington! It so reminds me of all the emotional investment and unhappiness involved, especially for women, when they try to establish a special relationship with any male guru or priest. They know—certainly Alison knows— with her head—that this is an unworthy way for two people with a similar religious commitment to be going on. But this system of guru devotion can leave a lot of people open to it. Also, as far as I can see, a lama is a law unto himself, with no one to whom he is responsible within a particular lineage. This is only a small wave of disharmony but it will be interesting to see if it occurs in other contexts later on. I do not believe that it can be very good for lamas any more than it is good for priests— both always men—to have the kind of power implied by a commitment of "complete obedience to the guru". Spiritual power must be as dangerous in Buddhism as in any other religion. From things that other people have said I pick up the destructive implications of this particular kind of rivalry. The only person, besides his mother, who seems unaffected by this desire to please the great man is Anila, who continues with her work as usual. He is, after all, only her little brother and his relationship with this solid and supportive woman must mean a lot in the tensions of his life.

I helped with painting some of the elaborate carved woodwork on the *gompa* door—a good bright red—while initiating a conversation with the Spanish nun. She is tense and highly strung. Also she is very thin for a Spanish woman of her age. We talked about places in Spain which I knew, like Alaurine el Grande where she had lived and where her father still has a house and where my daughter has lived also. She was clearly pleased by this European connection and seemed warm and friendly. But then I am not a Buddhist. When my bit of the painting was finished I walked across the courtyard to the kitchen to help make the potato *momo*s for lunch. These are small dumplings made of potato pasta and filled with chopped spinach before being steamed over a great pot on Anila's fire. There I learnt from Alison that yesterday she had been locked out of the cave by the Spanish nun and that today she had been locked in! Alison was quite prepared to laugh about it, aided in this approach by Merry and Harry, who were also there checking on all the preparations. By this afternoon there was still no news of any arrivals, so let's hope the elastic gets even slacker and some of the personal frustrations disappear in the general disappointment.

June 4 is another of the personally poignant days for me: the day on which Tabitha, my second daughter, was born, very easily and quickly, early in the morning. I had been exceptionally busy the day before and was not expecting her for another three or four days. All her life she was such an easy and happy baby. Charlotte and Toby, her sister and brother, were thrilled with her, and lying on my bed after feeding her I would talk and play with her as she smiled and gurgled away so responsively. It was 1947, an exceptionally hot summer. She would lie in her pram with only a little vest on and got quite brown and chubby. Then on August 27, when she was nearly three months old, I went out to fetch her from her pram after I had given the other two their lunch, and there, sticking out from below the thin cotton sheet, which was all she had covering her, were her little feet—quite blue. Almost fainting I snatched her up and ran to the telephone to get the doctor. I could hardly stand. I knew she was dead, for she was all limp and floppy in my arms. No kind of resuscitation worked. Now whenever I hear of a "cot death"—an unexplained death in early infancy—my heart gives a kind of thump and I see those little blue feet. I never had another daughter.

Of course I am crying as I write this. I am weeping for Tabitha

Mary on her birthday—who will always live in my memory as the adorable happy baby with the large brown eyes, but who might have been forty-three today. Is it a comfort to be a Buddhist and to think of her being born as someone else's baby—or as what? What form of enlightenment or merit has such a small spirit to guide it into another life? Or who—or what—in Buddhism does the guiding or choosing?

As I wonder about her all these questions about reincarnation crowd into my mind. If the questions could stay rooted in this culture they would not multiply so quickly. Even so, when I think of the bright-eyed little boy brought a year or so ago from the Spanish mountains to Nepal to fulfil a newly discerned lama life, this remains within a beneficent Buddhist culture. But I am distressed by the thought of the thin little Buddhist girls in Bangkok who believe they have to work for years as prostitutes to make amends for sins in a previous life. They are being exploited by the sinister manipulation of this belief.

Or is reincarnation a continuous spiritual process, or flow, of re-embodiment? God, I believe, is a spirit and that spirit moves within each one of us. Spirit is not bounded by our space-time box, needs no justification in terms of worth, flowing back into the fullness and ground of *being*. Retaining awareness, attaining peace—who knows? This is the great mystery of death which we are wise not to constrain within man-made systems of interpretation. For those who are left after the death of a tiny creature, so much loved, the difficulty is not so much coming to terms intellectually with the mystery, because the mystery of birth is so close, but letting go of the loving. I was in no way prepared for it. I went into a semi-frozen state, neglecting my two other small children because all love seemed to have died with her. Tim helped us all survive, but I am sure the other two were permanently affected and this was partly my fault, because I could not let her go.

After writing this I turned to one of Tim's arrangements of the *Upanishads* (6:19 Maitri):

> There is something beyond our mind,
> which abides in silence within our mind.
> It is the supreme mystery beyond thought.
> Let one's mind and one's subtle body rest upon that
> and not rest on anything else.

Then I went out into the cloud which hovered round the mountainside and picked some trails of clematis montana, bright yellow berberis flowers and a fully-opened giant spurge and put them in the jam jar at the base of my shrine for my baby's birthday. I was physically warmed by my walk for flowers. After arranging them I went to see old Amala, who is sad that her son, the Lama, is not coming. I gave her a dark red jersey —a Buddhist colour—with a warm hood. I hope she will use it.

It is seven o'clock. The dark is heavy around us. The birds have ceased their twittering, for long ago they found perches for the night. The sound of the bells on the two dzos has also tinkled into silence. They have been milked and will be lying chewing the cud, their thick coats damp with cloud-mist, in the courtyard. I have nothing to do but sit and watch my small wavering candle flame. A while ago I fed the base of it on the candle-holder rim with some wax which had fallen onto the piece of stone on which it balances. This wax is now all melted round the candle stump, making the wick flaccid so that it has fallen over on its side. Lying like this it does not give out enough light to read by, so I sit and watch it, listening to the silence throbbing around us. Any sound of dripping water or crackle of timber is quickly absorbed by the cloud in which we are suspended. I wonder how long the melted wax will continue to feed the wavering flame, with which I identify. All that has been given me in life is like this small reservoir of wax, of energy, enabling the uncertain flame to make its feeble mark in the darkness. While it gives light it is consumed.

Chapter 24

Churn and pestle and mortar

Tuesday 5 June

During one of the many times I woke in the night, engaged in the endless
battle of the fleas, trying not to scratch and going over in my mind how, as
someone very allergic to all insect bites, I could have been so stupid as to
come without a strong insect repellent, I was suddenly lifted from the irrita-
ting small world of my sleeping-bag by the awareness of strong moonlight
in the room. I have seldom experienced this up here because of the heavy
cloud at night. It stretched across the floor in a wide band from the window,
silhouetting the few simple objects in its path. I got up and looked out to
see that the nearly full moon was riding over the summit of Kwangde
accompanied by a single outrider star. Nyung Na takes place here at the full
moon of the summer solstice, an auspicious time—which will be on Friday.

   After quietly centring and breathing before my meditation this
morning, this prayer came, in perfect clarity, from somewhere at the back
of my head:

> O Thou, who art the light of the minds that know Thee,
> the strength of the wills that serve Thee
> and the joy of the souls that love Thee;
> help us so to know Thee that we may truly love Thee
> and so to love Thee that we may truly serve Thee;
> whom to serve is perfect freedom.

Enlightened mind—open mind—compassionate mind: the essence of
Buddhism.

Ian the doctor returned from the festival at Thami this morning, and Cathy had gone on back to the hospital at Khunde. To everyone's great delight he took the drainage tube out of the lady's leg and though there is still quite a hole, it looks much better. All this was caused by a vicious dog which has bitten five other people. Some Sherpas are not unlike certain people at home who think it is a sign that you are tough yourself if you have a fierce dog. Ian, hoping to hear some of Lama Zopa's teachings, is going to stay on for Nyung Na. He tells me he finds it very hard to meditate or slow down. I can see that in addition to a commitment to his work he is quite a "driven" personality. Probably Cathy is more intellectual and better able to pace herself. They have been reading the Enneagram book together and working on their personality differences with it—interesting that it has reached these remote heights! They stayed on with the Thami Lama last night, who is also suffering from fleas. I had pity on his old age and donated a very small amount of my remaining Betnovate cream in an old envelope, to be taken down to the village by the leg-lady's children. Ian says he can replace it from the hospital but, alas, that will not be possible before my departure. I hope the miserable remains will last me out. It won't if I have another attack like last night.

Just before lunch Sangay, the Lama's brother, and two other Sherpas arrived with the news that Lama Zopa will be here tomorrow—just in time for the beginning of Nyung Na. Amala was visibly pleased, talking to the young men in her funny old voice, in which the mutter becomes more high-pitched as she pulls the string of her prayer wheel. Anila gave us all lunch together in the big room, and Amala clearly revelled in the company. I'm afraid that the cosy days of kitchen meals are over. It will be interesting to see if some of the attitudes change too. Ian, with his local knowledge of the lamas round here and their health problems, is moving Alison—who in her religious attitudes shows unquestioning devotion—to assessing some of these attitudes more selectively. I enormously admire her constancy to the ordinary Sherpa way of life and belief, though I still feel it is not disloyal to recognize that such a type of devotion as is expected of them raises many questions for Westerners. I suspect that when Lama Zopa comes different attitudes may emerge which will clarify some things for me and which may also sort the snobs among the followers from the local faithful. In another way it is interesting for me, as I discern the tightening of the elastic again. I perceive that devotion to the idolization of compassion—Chenrezi—in an extremely personal way. This personal aspect of the devotion involved in all the visualizations of tantric Buddhism is perhaps the one where it differs most from other more philosophical and ethical Buddhist schools.

Drolkar is also back, having been allowed yesterday to go off to the Thami festival. She was disturbed and upset when she thought she might have to miss it because of the amount of work which still had to be done here. One of the Thamo nuns came up to lend a hand to enable her to go. This indicated a real understanding of a young girl's feelings. For it is one of the rare occasions when Drolkar can enjoy being with her brother and sisters, who live in Thami, in a festive atmosphere. "Pen!" she said, as she came through my door early with my breakfast. "Look, hairbands like a rainbow"—turning three of them in her hands to show me. She was so excited; bringing my breakfast had been a good way to share it. So Anila must also have given her a little money to spend. Every time we speak, her English improves. She is so bright and has such a need to communicate.

Recent acquisitions for the festivities have been four dried sheep's quarters, bought from a Tibetan trading woman who walked over the mountains with them hung over her shoulders. They are now hanging from the roof of the kitchen lobby. Sherpas and Tibetans are not strict vegetarians like other Buddhists. I imagine that the harsh conditions of their lives make it inevitable that they should eat anything available to sustain themselves. I am not sure though whether they would deliberately slaughter animals for food or just eat the ones that happen to die from other causes! This would be consistent with their admirably frugal outlook.

Also from the same trader Anila bought another block of compressed Tibetan tea. I think this must be the tea used in Tibetan butter tea. It has to be boiled in water a long time and then churned in a tall narrow wooden churn with a wooden plunger. This is quite hard work and produces something nearer a rather salty soup than the European idea of tea. Anila's churn is beautifully carved, is over a hundred years old and, she delights to recount, has never been washed. Her big wooden pestle and mortar is about the same age and equally untouched by water. Yesterday Alison recorded an interview with Anila for the BBC about her utensils, about Sherpa food and its preparation and the customs attached to it. There was much laughter as Anila described Sherpa cooking processes. "Every year coming, picking, then smashing." Alison: "Grinding with stone?" "Yes. Then cooking, then again smashing." Alison, laughing: "More smashing?" "Yes, many times smashing." Then they turned to cheese-making, Anila saying: "First milk taking, cooking, then keeping." "How long keeping?" asked Alison. "When good smell come," replied Anila. During these exchanges I discovered that the odd gobs of butter sticking to the top of the post supporting the kitchen ceiling were kept there to use for softening leather such as boots or the straps which secure a heavy load across the forehead. Merry and Harry acted as studio assistants on this occasion, and there was a lot more laughter when Anila tried to describe all the long-winded processes through which the production of *tsampa* is achieved. Tomorrow I am going to take some photos of Anila and her churn.

I have just been up towards the eastern *stupa*, my favourite stretch of this mountain. After a heavy shower during the afternoon the sun had come through and everything smelt freshly of juniper. As the low evening rays turned the outline of the western mountains a deep red, they also lit up the raindrops on the bushes. The patches of lichen-covered rock gleamed in shades of rust and yellow, while still-dripping swags of clematis climbed over all the wind-bent trees. Between the rocks, spears of irises thrust up their pale green blades and around them in clumps, the violets' heads drooped with moisture. I looked up at the ridge behind me, the highest point of my feeble explorations and thought how many more thousands of ridges and valleys, fold upon fold, lay hidden in these amazing mountains. I shall never come here again and I do wish I had been able to see more. However, as well as the unknown beauty and potential of life in wild and hard places is the value of all the little things. That is something I have learnt from Zen—each moment has its own potential and gift. As I turned back towards the *gompa* the sun moved lower behind the western ranges, flattening out the gullies and

ravines in shadow and leaving the frozen slopes of the higher giants
glinting as if decorated with pink marble.

The glowing outline of these serene high peaks lifted my heart and
soul from the small and intimate beauty at my feet. I had a sense of them
pulling something upward out of my centre—a something which fuelled
and guided my search. It was a sense of holiness drawing me out of
myself into a union behind all nature. This experience was not new to me.
I had felt a similar uplift in my teens when walking between the rows of
over-arching trees which rose towards the sky like the aisles of some great
cathedral, in the woods near my home.

With the arrival of the Lama's brother the elastic has tightened again
and all activity has taken on a more serious note. Merry came over during
the afternoon to look at the structural state of the *gompa* with him. She is
obviously a considerable benefactress whose opinion is valued. I had
previously discussed the whole question of the soil erosion with her: the
cutting of the trees and the grazing of the yaks. She is very conservation-
minded but being committed to this form of Buddhism, she is also
committed to these people and their culture. I guess that she does not
have to earn her living and this is her great cause. Do Americans need this
more than Europeans? Her manner is in some ways more, and in some
ways less, the concerned Westerner than Alison. It is most interesting to
watch them dealing with the issues in their very different ways. Merry is
perhaps more fatalistic than Alison, who has a lot of her mother's
practical application to achieving results as well as a lot of her cheerful
efficiency. Merry conceals her efficiency with more superficial chat while
working in a more oblique manner. Alison depends on Merry's support
and approval and Merry appears to depend on Harry's support. Merry is a
former Buddhist nun who has been, or is, married to a Frenchman with
whom she built her cave cell here. Harry is still a monk—of a very
relaxed American kind. At least while here she depends on his practical
advice as well as his religious judgement. He is kind and gentle and his
humour is certainly contagious and balanced. I wonder how close their
dharma has brought them in other ways?

Chapter 25

"May I be adorned with the excellent garment of patience" (Nyung Na text)

Wednesday 6 June

Sangay reported to us last night that ten days ago tanks had moved into Boudha (the place where Alison and I stayed before coming up here) because Communist elements were trying to organize a general strike. One of the major occupations in Boudha is working in the carpet factories. Most of the workers are Hindu Nepalis on very low wages and most of the employers are Tibetan Buddhists. Communal antagonism grew and the Nepalis started to smash the Tibetans' houses. I hope something will have been resolved by the time we get back there, which —weather at Lukla airstrip permitting—should be on the 12th. Also I hope the stuff we left at the Bir Hotel will be safe because the owners are Tibetans.

Preparations multiply here for the arrival of Lama Zopa and his party. A pink-cheeked, smiley old monk from the Thamo nunnery has come up and is repairing the large incense burner on the courtyard wall with clay. Alison continues with her painting of the courtyard doors and the Spanish nun has disappeared to her cell. Alison thinks she wants to be busy doing the remains of her painting when everyone arrives, because she needs the attention! The key commitment of tantric Buddhism—guru devotion—really does bring out the psychological bees from the bonnet. For she is not alone in this need. I suppose that many Westerners are looking for "alternative" guru figures to help solve their problems, having found priests, shrinks and psychotherapists inadequate. Others, where loyalty is part of their temperament, are looking for something worthy of that loyalty—probably having rejected, again as inadequate, the conventional objects of loyalty of their upbringing, such as family, class, political party, church or social peer group; perhaps they may just be people whose experience has given them a low self-image, and who feel this lack of confidence and self-esteem is the fault of our post-Christian society as they experience it. I meet people coming from all these places in my own counselling and spiritual work. My hope is to guide them towards that self-confidence which will allow them to trust their own judgement: to move them towards experiences which will validate their own abilities to grow and mature both psychologically and spiritually. I also meet people who have what one anthropologist calls the romantic Rousseau syndrome. They drop out from Western society looking for other cultures and beliefs because they find their own too structured. However, the reason they often feel freer in their adopted system is that they are not really inside it. For someone inside, it is likely to be as structured or hierarchical as the one they have left.

This initial insistence on dependence on the guru is part of the structure of Tibetan Buddhism which you have to accept if you want to get inside it. It is a necessary expression of commitment to this particular "way". But, as more *dharma* students who are at this stage arrive among us, I must not focus on the disadvantages of the system. For, after all, both Merry and Harry are mature and fairly disengaged products of it, and Norbu, though I am sure he is obedient to his abbot at Kopan, has a degree of autonomy up here which would be rare for a monk in the West. Dependency relates to decision-making and is not the same as religious devotion. Devotion—*bhakti*—wherever I encounter it in the world fills an important emotional need and is a vital initial response to the awareness of transcendence or a source of enlightenment, but it needs balancing with the critical discernment of the mind. In Moses' first encounter with the great "I Am," his enquiring mind was the initial response which prompted him to turn aside and investigate the bush which burned but was not consumed. Awareness of the sacred and removing his shoes followed. Whether a sense of the holy or a need to investigate comes first, for me the two aspects of the encounter cannot be split and for me any "way" I follow must combine them.

2:30pm

It has been a beautiful sunny morning. An excited Norbu, in his clean robe—washed in a bucket of rainwater after a recent storm and put to dry in the sun on the matting of the kitchen roof—and in his best red anorak, was off with the yak to Namche to meet Lama Zopa. The Thamo monk is now using his clay to make small *torma*s— offering figures. All the women are cleaning and cooking, and the young Thamo nun who arrived to replace Drolkar is still here. She has just taken the small green towel, which has hung on a nail on the kitchen post and been used for wiping hands, dishes, benches, shelves and even the floor, to give it a wash for the first time since I have been here. It looks quite a different green as it dries on one of the walls! I think, from her expression, that even she was a bit horrified at the colour of the successive rinsing waters that she alone had the right to use on it, as she had herself carried all the water up from the pipe earlier in the morning. I too had hung out some washing and bedding to be aired on the trees behind the *gompa*. All this activity as well as the colours of the drying garments and the fresh paint on the gates and on the *gompa* give the place a jolly, festive appearance.

The Thamo nun, Ian the doctor and I set out to join Sangay and another at the blind lama's cave. I encouraged them both to go ahead of me because I wanted to take advantage of the sun to photograph some flowers. I knew it would be a long session with the old man in the cave and I had already paid my respects, so I stayed on the mountain. They, in fact, stayed for a meal, so I was thankful for my decision and climbed gradually higher up the mountainside. As I crossed the various descending streams more and more varieties of primula were in bloom, from the deep mauve Wanda to many of all sorts and colours that I had never seen before. However, the tall and graceful single-flowered yellow one is still my favourite. There were also pale pink gentians, small rock roses and a miniature orange spurge as well as the big yellow one. I also found a white ling pushing up between the rocks and a tiny species of flowering sedge. Up here the juniper hugs the ground and the white clematis climbs all over it as a background to the jewel-like flowers, so that each hollow becomes a natural garden. My spontaneous response to such a place would be to lie on the ground embracing it all, or to roll in delight on the undergrowth, as I have on the Yorkshire or Scottish moors. Here, alas, in spite of the impulse to do this the ground is too wet, so I had to remain primly upright. As I came back along the steep path a cuckoo called loud and clear—the first I have heard here. Surely, I thought, it must be rather high for him.

The *gompa* almost waits on tiptoe for the first sign or sound of the Lama Zopa Rinpoche, who has not visited here for two years. In the quiet of my cell I meditated on a very different spiritual guide, Julian of Norwich. Her picture is the last of the cards on the wall of my windowsill shrine to be used in this way. I feel sure she would have understood the people whose lives I am sharing. For those she called her "even Christians", life was not unlike life here. The people of Norwich and round about, who came to her for counsel, had survived several epidemics of the plague as well as the Peasants' Revolt. The harvesting of food, the gathering and chopping of firewood and the drawing of water were all hard manual jobs for the survivors, as they are here. Julian's small cell was about the same size as mine and was built against the wall of the church in Rouen Lane. Rather in the same way that meals are carried from the kitchen to the hermits and retreatants here, Julian had women to look after her basic needs. We all know from her will that at one time one of them was called Alice and another Sarah. There were two windows or doors to her cell, one looking into the church so that she could see the celebration of the Mass and one through which she talked to those who visited her.

I have no copy of the *Revelations of Divine Love* with me, but I remember so well how Julian described her "showings"—as she called them—which took place while she was very ill and expected to die. I think something of the impulse and psychological preparation for this experience has been made clearer for me here. Our Western twentieth-century minds are so often shut off from the reality of bodily pain and suffering. We have effectively distanced ourselves from twisted bodies and seeping blood, by keeping them aseptic in hospitals or by seeing them as taking place somewhere else, as on our TV screens. For the thirteenth century this was not possible, and Julian's contemporaries would not have felt that slight sense of shocked incomprehension that accompanied my first reading of her account of her deep desire to know, in herself, the pain of Jesus' crucifixion. In all my reading of Buddhist texts I have never found one which does not suggest identification with beautiful, pure and peaceful images. Surely identification with "compassion" must include the dark and painful too? Indeed suffering, as the basic condition of life, is constantly talked about in Buddhism, but as something to avoid rather than as something transformative. All Julian's sufferings during her illness and her subsequent reflections on them were influenced by her understanding that her desire was being granted and that through that understanding she was better able to comprehend the nature of God.

In the hazelnut God showed her how he perpetually creates and sustains the world through love. He also showed her how human freedom involves being tried and "tempest-tossed" but never overcome, because of this sustaining love. She comes closer to Buddhist thought when she writes that sin "has no substance" and is known only by the pain it causes. Her understanding is that God is like a mother who picks us up, with no condemnation or blame, each time we fall as stumbling children. Her identification with all that she understood through her showings was brought to fruition in the following fifty years of her life, as she made herself available to all who came to her for counsel and, through her prayer, to the rest of the world. She has long been an inspiration and model for me of a certain kind of down-to-earth wisdom and a gift of feminine intuition made available to all. She is also an example of an educated, intelligent woman whose own experience led her to the contemplative prayer of silence and solitude, in response to these gifts of God's grace, but who never withdrew from the world in such a way as to cut herself off from ordinary people or the social, domestic and economic life of her time. As I sit in my cell, my strange retreat drawing to a close and so soon to be overtaken by the celebration of Chenrezi—the Buddha of Compassion—I think of Julian in her cell and, through her, I begin to understand a bit better the purpose of identification with this aspect of the historical Buddha.

All my dissent, my doubts and questionings of this form of Buddhism begin to seem excessive as I look back on them. However, they have been part of my experience here which I do not wish to repudiate. Perhaps it would have been better if I had had a guru of my own to consult, helping me to keep them in perspective. Julian has acted in this way for me before, and now I like to feel her companionship across time and space. Her homely God was mediated to her through the compassion of Christ—"Our Lord takes our strivings and sends them up to heaven," she wrote; and my ultimate trust is strengthened by her faith that we are "body and soul clad and enclosed in the goodness of God."

As the evening draws on, more and more Western *dharma* students arrive with their backpacks, as well as people from the villages in the valley. But no Lama. No plane was able to come in to Lukla yesterday, so Nyung Na celebrations will have to start without him. There is a sense of sadness and disappointment in the family. The abbot from Thamo will lead the proceedings, and before the evening *puja*—the first *puja* any of our little core group here will have had together—the Spanish nun will give a talk, in English, to the uninitiated. None of the visiting Westerners seem to have been here for Nyung Na before. I have already talked to a nice Swedish girl, who could not understand a Christian being in such a place. "But Christians do not meditate," she said—illustrating my sense of the uninformed criticisms of Christianity. "In the Church of Sweden all they do is sing and pray, which just means asking God for things, not seeking responsibility and enlightenment." I have also talked to an American, who has been running a physiotherapy course in Kathmandu. Most of her students are Hindus, some of them Brahmins who do not want to touch low-caste patients. All of them are interested only in getting qualifications for status and money, she says. She seems very disillusioned with Nepali society and enjoys getting up here to be among simple "uncontaminated" Buddhists.

The Spanish nun took us up to the cave *gompa* as it got dark to have our talk on Nyung Na. Just a few candles, the sloping rock roof, the Lama's throne-bed, flapping prayer flags in the small courtyard, the encircling evening mist and the diminutive Spanish nun with her shaved head sitting on the floor wrapped in her rust-coloured robes: all spoke more to me than her heavily accented words and rather conventional sentiments. This was followed by a marvellous meal on the benches in the big room. Westerners (called in Sherpa *Injies*, pidgin for English) and Sherpas all squashed together, about twelve on each side. I sat wedged between the case of Amala's big prayerwheel and a wrinkle-faced, animated old Sherpa with long hair, who turned out to be Norbu's father. Most of these old Sherpa men wear the Tibetan *chuva*, which is of dark woollen material like a wide smock, over narrow trousers. The *chuva* is belted at the waist and pouched over. They have a splendid variety of hats, often with wide brims, which they love to wear at a jaunty angle, and then a jacket with one arm hanging down, hussar-style, like my mountain friend who wanted my boots.

There was an enormous amount of Sherpa stew in two vast pots, which needed two men each to carry them through from the kitchen. For the first time since I have been here there was meat in it—two of the dried quarters of sheep which had been hung up in the lobby. It was not as inventive as Anila's usual stews, and only the fat of the meat was discernible, but it made a different taste. Then we had a choice of butter, black or milk tea. Drolkar, knowing my tastes, brought me watered black, in a smart mug I had never seen before. Where Anila has been hiding all that was needed for this feast I cannot imagine. Perhaps a lot of it has been borrowed, as this is a big event for the whole area and tomorrow we move into a long fast. It was therefore quite a solemn occasion with no *rakshi*, but it was all very relaxed: the weather-beaten and lined faces twinkled readily with smiles in the candlelight. When conversation flagged no one worried. They just sat and moved their fingers round their *malla* beads and prayed. I was delighted to see so many local people, though they were mostly the old and middle-aged.

As the meal came to an end, Cathy came up from Khunde hospital to join us. She was very warmly greeted as she slipped her pack off her shoulders. She and Ian plan to stay for the ceremonies. She has become very popular here, particularly with the Lawudo family and the family of the lady-with-the-leg. They respect her as a doctor and respond to her quiet way of relating to them. Before we went to our sleeping quarters round the *gompa* complex, two of the young monks with the Thamo

abbot set up their nine-foot-long horns on the courtyard wall and blew
them, to announce the beginning of Nyung Na to the people of the
valley. It was wonderful to hear the deep throbbing sounds I had heard in
the *gompa* echoing back from the distant walls of rock below Kwangde,
through the mist and night air which swirled around our guttering
candles and darting torches. How happy Norbu was to exchange this
sound of his lonely vigils for the real thing, as he moved among the
throng taking care of everything. He must be happy too to have the
monks sleeping with him now below me in the *gompa*, for I know that at
Lawudo he misses the companionship of other committed men which
he would enjoy in a larger community. He had warned me that I too
would have to share my cell with others tomorrow. For he knows that the
reverse has been true for me, my silence and solitude most precious. So I
went to bed thankful for four weeks of undisturbed peaceful occupancy
of my cell, filled with the smell of his incense, the thermos of hot tea
and other signs around me of the simple caring of Anila and Drolkar. I
think in that final talk at Bangkok before his death, Thomas Merton said
something about compassion being an awareness of the
interdependence of all living beings.

Chapter 26

Guru devotion

A beautiful sunny morning after so many days of mist. The place is abuzz with rumours. Would he come? Wouldn't he come? Norbu returned with the yak from an early visit to Namche and reported that a helicopter had been organized and that the eagerly expected Lama would arrive during the morning. Lookouts were posted on the wall of the courtyard with my binoculars, the two horn-playing monks got their great horns propped up on the parapet, as last night, to start blowing as soon as he appeared. Then gongs and smaller horns started up from within the *gompa* to warn us that the first session of the ceremonies was about to begin. These *puja* (prayer) sessions last about four hours. We will have three today and four tomorrow, fasting from food and drink. (I'm afraid I am going to break the drink fast. At this altitude I seem to need liquid.) The final session will be on Saturday morning, followed by special celebratory offerings.

The abbot of the Thamo monastery arrived with his enormous yellow headdress, which reminds me of some of the high ceremonial helmets on Assyrian reliefs. The abbot and his chief assistant monk will

• *View from the cave roof: the house, kitchen and gompa*

overleaf: • *Announcing the start of Nyung Na and the Lama's arrival by helicopter*
• *The abbot from Thamo*

lead all the *puja* and the monks and nuns from the surrounding monasteries are supporting them. We were just getting into the chanting when there were shouts from outside and at the same time a helicopter engine could be heard throbbing up the valley. Activity and excitement exploded around me, especially among the Western devotees. Armed with cameras, *kata*s (a small white cotton scarf given as an offering of respect, which is then blessed and returned to you), flowers and swinging censers, everyone shot off down the mountainside. Meanwhile the silver helicopter circled the only possible landing place, one of the little flat fields of Mende, some distance from the path. There was then a real scramble across the low stone walls to be the first to get to the throbbing silver bird which was bearing the object of everyone's devotion. From the courtyard wall, as I looked down on it all, it was much more like the arrival of a film star than anything else. There was even a French girl with a film camera right up front with Alison. The music that accompanied the Lama's landing was, however, totally Tibetan, dominated from where I stood by the great horns throwing out their booming sound across the valley to the peak of Kwangde, while beside me the clay incense burner, as large as a garden urn, sent spirals of smoke into the air.

From where I stood the red-robed figure and his assistant who climbed out of the helicopter looked diminutive as they were surrounded by the buzzing crowd. Peter emerged to hold a large red umbrella over the Lama, and the colourful procession began the steep twisting route back up the mountain. As the helicopter engines revved up and it took off like an awkward stork, circled the Mende fields and was gone, the excitement twisted back up the mountain track in waves. The procession included helpers carrying luggage, monks with offerings, an old Sherpa with a swinging censer and the abbot in his great feathered gold headdress. Ian, supporting Amala, had gone to a vantage point at the top

• *North face of the Kwangde range, with early-morning shadow of the mani stone*

previous page:
• *Lama Thubten Zopa Rinpoche talking to me*
• *The cave where the previous Lawudo Lama lived*

of the path. I joined them there as a good place for photographs. Ian kindly gave me a *kata* to offer, something I had never thought of acquiring for myself. As Lama Zopa, with his entourage, came up to the stretch of flat path before the *gompa* gates, he greeted his mother as she bowed and offered him the *kata*. Her dear old wrinkled face was full of contentment. Then someone introduced Ian as the Khunde doctor, and after their exchange of the *kata* he looked at me and said, "Are you a doctor too?" I replied, "No, I am a Christian retreatant, very grateful for the hospitality of Lawudo," and gave him the *kata*, which he blessed and put round my neck. Everyone seemed pleased and happy with these exchanges, and I felt grateful at that moment for the acceptance by them all. I remembered our previous meeting in London, when he came with Lama Thubten Yeshe. I recognized his rather serious expression, but on this occasion it quickly turned to smiles.

Everything has now changed gear. The intimacy of kitchen meals, the times for a simple exchange of words and the sense of a small family group has been overtaken. The serious business of Nyung Na is in full swing. In the *gompa* the Lama sits on his throne by the main altar with its garishly painted statues with eyes like marbles. Between the altar and the main door the monks and nuns sit in rows on each side: monks to the right, nuns to the left. Other men are behind the monks and most women behind the nuns, though many older Sherpa women sit on benches against the outer wall. Ano, the eight-year-old son of the lady-with-the-leg, who has been a great worker and water-carrier, comes to each session and joins the men immediately behind the monks. Is this a sign of vocation? I sit far to the left on a mat, with my back against the wall. Round me Western women try to follow the *puja* with their texts resting on pieces of material in front of them, for it is disrespectful to put sacred texts directly on the ground. As the day draws on they show their origins and personalities in a strange variety of dress and have around them an odd assortment of rugs, sleeping-bags, hats and scarves to guard against the sudden night cold. I can look beyond them to the backs of the shaved heads of the nuns in their dark robes and gathered cloaks. One of them presides over a great green drum hanging from a rafter and another has a big conch shell. The Sherpas beyond them, all in traditional dress, their *malla*s in their hands, have no texts. Is this because the ritual has not yet been translated from Tibetan into Sherpa, or is it because they cannot read anyway?

During a lot of the proceedings the Lama moves his body in time to the chanting and rhythmically rings his bell. The translated text, while the light lasted, helped me to follow what was going on.

> Guru is Buddha, guru is *dharma*, guru is *sangha* also,
> guru is the creator of all happiness, to all gurus I go for refuge.
> I will generate the enlightenment thought in order to attain success
> for myself and all other living beings.

Each invocation is chanted three times, and these three invocations seem to begin each *puja*. The last certainly implies some God-like qualities and powers for the Buddha, but I have been determined not to approach these celebrations in an analytical comparative-studies mode and tried to take in what followed at a different level. There were many expressions of commitment, of prayers to the lineage-lamas, of blessing of offerings and a lot of visualizations all involving long descriptions of what is to be visualized and how to appropriate it, which gives the feel of the spiritual climate which is generated. Needless to say, even in following the details of some of the visualizations, I retain a certain resentment at being told exactly what I should feel—even though I really entered into doing them.

Because the Lama is with us, apparently many extra *puja*s are included in the proceedings, which makes them even longer. We had one of these to "the protectors" on this first evening. If I had not been getting so cold I could really have let myself go into this, for it was not unlike Norbu's day of *puja* in the *gompa*, the sound of which below my cell had pulled me into my own kind of involvement in this unique expression of devotion. As it was, it was long after nightfall by the time it ended and only then did the Lama begin to teach. In the large high building, sitting quite still, I had not realized how much I would feel the damp cold around us. My attention level had dipped pretty low and it went even lower at the style of his delivery. This is sad, because I have read good translations of his meditations in various Buddhist publications and found them truly illuminating and helpful.

Born on this side of the valley, as a child he was always trying to climb up to the cave where the previous lama had lived. This old man had been looked after by Amala until he died. When five years old it was decided that Zopa was the reincarnation (*rinpoche*) of this lama, and he was taken off to Tibet to be educated. As a result of this Lama Zopa has not retained his native Sherpa tongue and so spoke to the local people in Tibetan, which had then to be translated for them by Norbu. Norbu was excellent at this task, because though the Lama remained rather solemn and was continually coughing and clearing his throat, Norbu, while apparently keeping to the substance of the talk, spoke with greater fluency and often made the local people laugh. I wanted to laugh too because by this point I could see this double act only as a kind of *Beyond the Fringe* skit of a guru session. It is not difficult to make fun of this kind of language any more than of any other religious language. But I kept a solemn face for the sake of my friends.

Halfway through this teaching it became apparent that, though the Westerners had been promised something in English—which Lama Zopa speaks well—it was getting too late for this to happen after the Sherpa version. It was already 10:30 and though in India he teaches into the early hours of the morning, he and most of the people here had had long and arduous journeys that day. His English-speaking attendant Pemba suggested English-speakers should all sit on one side and he would translate for us quietly as the teaching proceeded. This he did, having to wait for long intervals for the coughing, throat-clearing and repetitions. I was also deeply disappointed with the content. Cathy and I agreed the next day that if someone had spoken in such a way, with regard to both delivery and content, in the West we would have got up and left. Perhaps some of the repetitiousness was considered important with this Sherpa audience—in which case I think this was an insult to them. What is the source of this hero-worship? I suspect that Lama Zopa is warm and perceptive when he sees people individually and I know that his schedules for doing this round the world would kill most people. In any case I think I decided this evening that I could take in his teaching much more effectively from a good printed translation. As Pemba faltered and the whole thing dragged on I wondered further about this guru devotion. Were first-century Palestinians as uncritical in this way about Jesus? Perhaps the large crowds were. Perhaps the psychology of all crowds is a diminution of the critical faculties? Maybe only Jesus' close friends like Martha, scolding him for not coming sooner to the dying Lazarus, had the courage to question him. Perhaps it is therefore because I have not spoken intimately with Lama Zopa that I miss something essential in his charisma? In any case I had to make another of these decisions, that next day I would move out of my head and let the *puja* flow over me at a different level. I remembered a proverb: "The nearer you are to the Buddha, the more flexible you can be."

Through all my mental questioning, through the evidence of all my prejudices, which I hoped I had left behind, my varied experiences of the last month have left me more than enough to reflect on. I come back again and again to the thankfulness I feel for this place and these people, both Sherpa and Western, who have made my life here such an important stage on my own spiritual pilgrimage. Earlier, as the afternoon *puja* came to an end and the people filed out of the *gompa*, the low afternoon sun picked out all the bright paintwork of the buildings and the colours of the people's clothes. The atmosphere was serious but happy; a mood of commitment and community was evident in the weather-beaten faces. I walked up the mountain and looked down on the bright scene: the Mende children playing, the old ladies lifting up their skirts to squat behind the juniper bushes, Drolkar milking the dzo by the kitchen door, Norbu and Ano carrying water through to Anila, the men and the monks sitting and talking quietly on the *gompa* wall; and the sun, yet again descending behind the western ranges, edged Khumbila's snow-capped height in gold.

Chapter 27

"The nearer you are to the Buddha the more flexible you can be"

I woke after a restless night sharing my cell with an American woman who ran a *dharma* centre in Idaho and a very serious and devout Spanish girl. The American blew her nose and coughed a lot during the night, complaining of a cold which had been going round the *dharma* students at Kopan. The Spanish girl, Maria, left the room at about midnight and I discovered today that she had spent the whole night in meditation in the *gompa*. I felt bad because they were both in sleeping-bags on the floor and I was on the only bed. I also felt confused by the muddle the American had created round herself, with a profusion of trekking clutter in what had been *my* cell! Perhaps it is this, as well as the long cold evening at the ceremonies, which has given me a sore throat. I certainly have one.

To reduce my feeling of a loss of control over my environment, which I am not being very detached about, I did most of my packing and in consequence missed a part of the early *puja* where the faithful take the vows not to eat or drink for twenty-four hours. So when I went to the kitchen to get some breakfast I told Anila I would not be fasting. There were a number of others in the same boat, some with sore throats, but I did feel for a bit that it was a kind of cop-out, because things were changing so much around me. However, on reflection, I knew that my past experience of fasting left me with no need to prove anything to myself and it was for myself that I needed to take sensible decisions. My primary commitment was not to a group who happened to have gathered for the ceremonies at the end of my time at Lawudo; I needed to be strong the following day to begin the descent—I had some anxieties because of my experiences on the way up and the weakness of my left knee. But I did join in some part of all the sessions, particularly some of the extra *puja*s where the need to keep up with the text seemed less important and I could join in the prostration in my own way and with my own thoughts which linked them to the ending of my retreat. This was just as well, as at an early session I lent my English text to a Danish girl who looked thoroughly lost. This text was subtitled *The Sadhana according to Gelongma Palmo of the Great Compassionate One*— Gelongma Palmo was a woman *bodhisattva*—and the text had been translated by Merry. I never saw it, or the Danish girl, again. Maybe she, like the Swede I had talked to on the first day, had found it too strange to take. Yesterday the Swede had told me she was leaving. Perhaps the Dane had also trekked back to Namche this morning taking my text with her. The instructions in the text are important because in this tradition of *puja*—prayer—as in many different Buddhist traditions, each worshipper is expected to be envisaging the same thing. So when the text demands it and the worshippers chant, the *puja* has a focused communal quality.

I was certainly finding the contrast between the marvellous partial silence and solitude of the last weeks and these public ceremonies in the tantric Tibetan tradition a bit difficult to hold together. The repetitive chanting of the texts seems primarily the responsibility of the Thamo abbot and his nuns. From their strong faces I can tell that these nuns are women of character. Their features seem accentuated by their shaven heads. They also have strong voices, mostly in the mezzo-soprano or alto range, and they sing with no suggestion of tonal variation. The monks and the rest of the congregation follow their lead, when they know the chants. I finally decided to hum the themes I grew familiar with because I did not know the Tibetan words. The musical phrases always ended in the same way and the general affect is not unlike plainchant. Each section of text seems to be brought to an end when the abbot clashes his cymbals. The monks then blow their short horns, a nun beats the large drum suspended from the rafter and another nun blows the conch shell. I wish I knew the symbolism of all this. Many bells are also rung. This splendid period of sound lasts for more than five minutes, during which I am able to abandon myself to the sensation of the overpowering noise.

After a short silence, at the tinkling of the Lama's bell, the chanting rhythm is taken up again. At certain moments in the ritual, symbolic *mudra*s (hand movements) are used, particularly by the Lama, holding his bell in one hand and his *dorje* in the other. The *dorje* is like a small bronze sceptre, representing the male principle, just as the bell represents the female. I noticed how graceful his *mudra*s were. I have some small silver versions of the bell and *dorje* on a coral necklace, bought in Bhaktapur. They certainly fit neatly into each other reminding one of sexual intercourse and emphasizing interconnectedness and non-duality. I noticed that Alison was the only devotee with a *dorje* and bell of her own. Early in the proceedings, the young monks facing me looked across to see where the soft ringing was coming from, for the *mudra*s should apparently be done in such a way that the bell remains silent. As their eyes located Alison I realized that the Lama's *dorje* and bell were the only other ones being used. They were certainly not displeased but I was not sure whether these smiles indicated what they thought of over-enthusiastic Western devotees, or whether it was just tolerance. Alison had previously said something to me about being allowed to use them because they were borrowed. I still do not understand the significance of this or how anyone else was supposed to know it. Merry, sitting beside her, was certainly without them. However, when they were used I found the *mudra*s gentle flowing symbols of non-duality.

Yesterday evening there had apparently been another casualty to the sore-throat infection. A young Frenchman, in a white suit and looking remarkably like Swinburne, had settled himself with his girlfriend on ours, the female side of the *gompa*. This morning he suddenly got up during a *puja* to the "protectors" and, looking really ill, staggered out of the door. Whenever I went into the big room after that he was sitting on a bench in the corner, wrapped in his sleeping-bag being ministered to by the lady-with-the-leg. He apparently also had a very upset stomach and looked totally miserable. I felt a certain amount of resentment about all this praying for the "protectors"—landlords and other categories of people often most insensitive to the "happiness of all sentient beings." Buddhism often has this appearance of subservience to the current status quo, giving it a bland aspect, limiting its message to ethics and personal growth, ignoring the social element. This is no more so, I suppose, than a good deal of the same kind of thing in Anglicanism, such as praying for the Queen or members of the government. I felt happier with the *puja* to the lineage-lamas. These thoughts were in and out of my head during the sessions in the *gompa* and then suddenly there would be a period of battering noise, which made any thought impossible, followed by prostrations.

Students, during their training, are set a target of hundreds or thousands of prostrations—doing them in the strangest places like cemeteries or railway stations, as well as at sacred sites. In the *gompa* there was not enough room for all of us to make full-length prostrations all at the same time, so I found myself a corner where I could kneel and bow to the ground in that position. I found these periods good, as involving my body more fully in my prayer and as helping to keep my intellectual questioning at bay. I found a Christian-Buddhist synthesis in using a phrase like "the light which lights everyone" and remembering also yesterday's conversation with Cathy when, discussing the different interpretations of compassion, she said she found her desire to be compassionate involved also a lot of pride. A Western doctor, in a society which needs what only she can provide, must be more open to this than most of us. I see genuine humility as an increasingly interior orientation which acts as a goad to true compassionate action.

During the afternoon I went for a short walk with Cathy and we sat beside the path to the water pipe discussing our responses to the Nyung Na experience. She rather resented Ian's attitude of personal devotion to Lama Zopa which he had shown when they had been granted an interview this morning with him in the cave. It seems to me that Ian is just identifying with all the Sherpas around him and it is in Cathy's nature to be more detached. Perhaps Cathy and I are not sufficiently aware of the diverse ways people are enabled to fulfil their *karma* through these experiences. But I did sympathize with how she felt, as it is so close to many of my feelings. I had wondered to myself whether I should ask

Pemba for a personal interview, but there were so many people anxious to see Lama Zopa and I had in mind particularly the local people, for whom this was a rare chance. It also seemed to me that he must need some time for himself between the long hours in the *gompa*. I had learnt from Sangay that he would stay in Kathmandu for a few days on his return and, as I now knew that I would be there during this time also, I planned to ask to see him then. It could be more fruitful. Here and now it seems that the pressure of Westerners' expectations are somewhat distorting on the relationships.

During the next *puja* our side of the *gompa*, having lost the Frenchman and his companion, acquired during the day some German visitors. They sat cross-legged just in front of me, a beautiful young blonde girl with a concentrated, serious expression and an older, bearded man who appeared more detached. Both inside the *gompa* and outside he was looking round curiously at everything and I wondered if he might be an anthropologist. There were further interesting ceremonies dispersed throughout the sessions. Blessed water was brought round and tipped into everyone's cupped hands by Norbu, Drolkar and other helpers. Those who were fasting, instead of drinking it when the signal was given, poured it on their heads. This seemed to occur about once a session as a symbol of purification. Blessed rice was also distributed in the same way and at a signal from the abbot, thrown on the ground or over your neighbour, symbolizing fertility and long life.

**"In this land walled round by snowy mountains
you are the source of all happiness and good"**   (Nyung Na text)

Saturday 9 June

In the early morning of the third day of the ceremonies the fast was over. During the *puja*s, which started at 4:30, the light crept up over the rim of Khumbila and started to filter through the *gompa* windows as we stopped in silence to have our first round of hot drinks. These were most welcome to me because by now I had lost my voice. I had forgotten to bring my tin mug from my cell to receive the pungent herb

tea, but Drolkar brought me one. From time to time during the four
hours of this *puja* session special food was also brought round in large
containers, one of which was my red plastic bucket which I had earlier
that morning given to Norbu for the purpose. He was delighted and
rushed off with it to the kitchen straight away. It was some kind of
thank-you present to him for bringing it up from Namche for me on the
yak. It had proved one of my most useful acquisitions, as a water
carrier, laundry basket, washbasin and, in emergency when it rained at
night, a loo.

On this last day of Nyung Na and my final morning at Lawudo I
felt sad and at the same time full of thanksgiving. I seemed to have put
down some roots in the place which were going to be hard to pull up. I
had also grown so close to these tough and sympathetic people. To keep
my midday rendezvous in Namche with Alison I had to allow that I
would take longer going down than she would. So I decided to miss the
final offering ceremonies. When the early-morning *puja* was over I went
back to my cell, now changed and somewhat alien. This made it easier
for me to do my final pack and shut the door on my home of the last
four weeks. The sunlight from the window filled it with familiar
shadows and it still smelt of Norbu's incense hung on the hook by the
door. Then with my pack on my back I went down to the kitchen. Anila,
with tears in her eyes, just took hold of me and said, as she often did,
"Oh sorry, Pen." I knew this time that she did not mean it because there
was no hot water, or that it was raining, or that I had fleabites, but
because I was leaving. "No 'sorry', Anila," I said—"Just thank you,
thank you." And she buried her shaven head in my shoulder and allowed
herself to cry for a moment.

At that point Sangay, the Lama's brother, came in and, putting a
kata round my neck, said, "Thank you for being here. Blessings for your
journey." I was most moved and went with him into the big room to eat
tsampa for breakfast. The ill Frenchman and his girlfriend were also there
being fed. Most people would not eat until the great feast after the
offering ceremonies. Local Sherpa women helpers were wandering in and
out looking relaxed and pleased that all had gone well and that their
culinary efforts would soon be offered in the *gompa*. I felt some regret
that I had decided not to stay for this final stage, when Anila came in

with a big bag of the traditional food offerings, which are like twists of sweet deep-fried pasta, quite like the snacks you buy from street stalls in Spain. This was her present for my journey. I was also further overcome by the lady-with-the-leg putting a *kata* round my neck and holding my hands affectionately as we bowed *"Namaste"* to each other.

Quite early in the morning, when it was still dark, I had taken another important farewell. As I heard Drolkar's soft singing to the dzos as she brought them into the courtyard for milking, I had slipped out of the *gompa* to say a peaceful goodbye to her and to give her my T-shirt and folding camping spoon and fork as a present. I just took her shoulders and wished her lots of happiness. "Sad you going," she said. This Nyung Na had been full of good new experiences for her. Merry had also said goodbye to me earlier, with promises to be in touch when next in London. I had managed to catch Harry and bid farewell to him also, and to Ian and Cathy. As I was telling Alison where I had left my big pack so that it could come down with her and the porter later, I saw the raven with the red tie, unperturbed by the crowds, keeping watch from the courtyard wall as usual.

Finally, shouldering my small pack, with my binoculars and camera in it, and my water bottle and hat, I went across to the old lady's corner and, bowing, clasped her hands. She smiled her toothless smile and patted my arm. As I retreated into the courtyard I made a general farewell *Namaste* to the big room and the familiar kitchen, now so full of bustling people, and was off. Crossing the courtyard on the uneven stones, I passed the *gompa* on my right. Ano was sitting on the steps listening to the chanting coming through the open doors. He had been put in charge of all the boots and shoes left in a pile there before people entered. He was proud of this responsibility because yesterday someone had lost a boot. With his bright dark eyes and glowing cheeks, he seemed a Sherpa symbol as he responded with a grin to my wave and *Namaste*. Passing through Alison's newly painted gates and leaving the carved *mani* stone on my right, I took the twisting rocky path downwards on the first stage of my return journey.

Chapter 28

The road back to Lukla

I moved down the mountainside in slow stages: first of all the steep path to the Mende *stupa*, where I ran my hand over all the carved *mani* stones at its base already warm in the sun, then a comparatively flat stage past the walled fields, followed by the next steep stretch up which I had climbed alone after my restorative sleep under the juniper bush. From this narrow path I looked down on the valley of the Kyajo Drangka, which I had watched as it fell down the mountainside from above the eastern *stupa*. I sat on a rock in the sun and looked back towards this favourite vantage point. It was so far off that if I had not known exactly where to look its grey stones would have appeared to be part of the surrounding rocky landscape. Immediately below me the stream wound through the village where my narrow path met the wider road from Namche to Thami. As I wound my way down I could see the yak trains and colourful groups of people returning west from the Namche Saturday market. I passed more and more of these as I crossed the bridge at Phurte and on into Namche to wait at the Lodge by the crossroads for Alison to join me for lunch. Sitting now on the low wall and watching all the life of this region passing below me I feel like getting up and shouting for joy at the wonderful experiences I have had since I last sat here.

Alison arrived with a rather squint-eyed young cousin of Norbu's carrying our packs. We agreed to meet him at Josale, and after a quick potato pancake we too moved off. I relied heavily on Tim's stick on the steeper sections of the path as we got down to the Hillary bridge and crossed over to turn south beside the confluent rivers. This crossing must be impressive after the monsoon. Now the water is low, which is just as well as our next crossing was the low bridge cantilevered out from the stones. Before we reached this we encountered another wild mountain character hopping over the stones in bare feet. His lined face, bright eyes and lithe body made it very difficult to tell what age he might be. He was in good spirits as he passed us, and just before the bridge we caught up with him again sitting drinking with three other rough-looking men round a fire which they had lit on the big flat stones at the edge of the river. They were cooking an animal of some kind on it. We thought they were probably poachers of musk deer.

When we reached Josale, the dark village where we spent the night on the way up, on the other side of the high suspension bridge we found Norbu's cousin waiting for us. I was surprised that I felt able to continue on to the next village before stopping for the night, but pleased that Alison had offered to give me some antibiotic this evening, as my sore throat has become a painful cough. She and our young porter have now gone ahead and I am resting near the National Park post, having delayed to take some photographs of two water mills housed in little wooden huts, which I had not noticed on the way up. There was a woman grinding barley in one of them, the bounding water turning the wooden clappers all the time with an uncertain rhythm. Across the valley there is a great leaping waterfall cascading down the mountainside which fills the whole enclosed narrow space with its roar. I have noticed that every now and again the water seems to gather itself inward for a brief second, as if drawing back over smooth rock and then with renewed vigour leaps out over the valley again in an arc of water and sound. Behind this arching curve of the torrent there must be some inner space of silence such as I had found at the heart of the battering music of Nyung Na.

We stopped the night at a lodge owned by one of Cathy's auxiliary medics. Our hostess gave us a simple meal as she was in a hurry to get off to the small *gompa* higher up the valley side where feasting after the Nyung Na fast would soon be coming to an end. Alison and Norbu's cousin decided to go with her. They left advising me to lock the door of my small wooden cubicle off the main dormitory. I am lucky still to have enough money to pay for this. As I write I can imagine that a lot of drinking and jollification is going on in all the villages of the Solu Khumbu tonight. So here I am alone again, in a small wooden cell in a house above the Dudh Kosi which I can hear pounding over its stony bed beyond the barley field. It seems a long day's walk from Lawudo but I feel quite relaxed in these remote places now among these cheerful strangers. Having taken one of Alison's antibiotic pills I hope for a sound sleep and less of a rough throat in the morning.

Sunday 10 June

Alison tells me that last night there was much dancing and singing as well as so much to drink that many people were unable to find their way home. I was sleeping the sleep of exhaustion and only dimly remember some shouting and knocking on our windows as the revellers returned. Tonight we are back at Apple Pie Lodge in Phakding. As our route led us up the steep rocky paths, across the bridges and along the village tracks that we had climbed four weeks ago in the opposite direction, I noticed how much greener the fields and the hillsides were. In many of the villages the barley and wheat were being cut by hand with small sickles and hay was being stacked beside the barns built against the stone houses. Here our hostess is alone and looking rather sad. Pemba, her son, and the schoolmaster have apparently gone to Kathmandu. She was subdued as she served our meal and we were not offered peach wine as before. Just as we had nearly finished eating, our rough barefooted friend and his mates came in with loud chatter and a rush of cold air. We exchanged a *"Namaste"* and laughed at the way our paths kept crossing. Our hostess grew visibly more cheerful. As Alison and I went off to bed I felt sure her lovely hair would be let down again. When I woke in the night to shouts and running footsteps I was glad I had my small room to myself. I got up and went into the dormitory which led off it. Alison was still asleep but Norbu's cousin had locked the door and had pulled his bed protectively across it. He grinned when I asked him to move— perhaps he did not realize that I needed a nightly visit to relieve my bladder. In the passage I met our hostess dishevelled and breathless in a long white nightdress. She looked surprised to see me and apologized for the noise. I patted her arm and said, "No matter." Alison had not stirred on my return and our protective young porter was clearly glad to see me. I guess it is this kind of house and anyway I also guess that the festivities and drinking go on for several days.

As we came down into Lukla in the late afternoon the orchards of apple and plum trees were coming into bloom. I realized how little of this gentle rolling landscape I had taken in on the way up because of my preoccupation with the towering heights which lay ahead of us. Alison went ahead to see if her friends at Thami Lodge would have room for us. I sat on a rock beside the path enjoying the peaceful scene in the sunshine and thinking how amazingly lucky I have been to make this expedition with such a good and patient friend. Alison, so much younger, stronger and experienced than I, could have got very fed up with my slow pace of progress and my critical remarks about a way of life so dear to her. I felt a trust that this time together, which has proved so important for me, has not impaired our friendship. As I entered the rather dirty village of Lukla itself it looked less grey and forbidding. Alison called in at Thami Lodge but they had no room for us. She was reluctant to go to the far side of the airstrip to find accommodation as these lodges were more Westernized. However, after trying a couple we decided on the one with the best view and washing facilities and the least smell of drains. Are we already changing our perspectives? From here we look out over the airstrip from which we should leave for Kathmandu tomorrow.

Chapter 29

Lukla

We have been here for two days waiting for a flight to Kathmandu. We are shrouded in cloud and the visibility is nil. Alison knows of people stuck here for more than a week. This situation certainly brings out all sorts of temperamental traits and eccentricities in the waiting travellers. The two main lodges near the airstrip house most of the Europeans hopeful for a flight. In ours—"The Himalaya"—until this evening there have been only participants from the Nyung Na festival at Lawudo. They are the Spanish girl Maria with a young Spanish monk Jose and Christian, the older German man, who is an economist with an international aid agency organizing a conference in Kathmandu, with his daughter Nikki. Maria is not prepared to enter into any discussion of our shared experiences but only to exchange admiring stories about Lama Zopa. Jose is stern and gaunt, the stuff from which missionaries and martyrs are made. He has recently been made a monk by Lama Zopa. Whether such ordinations follow some formal pattern of study and a time of preparation laid down by the lineage, or are simply authorized by the lamas from among their own followers, I have not been able to discover. However, he was prepared to risk his lack of fluency in English to enter into a serious discussion with Nikki, who appears to be a practising Catholic. His main argument was that tantric Buddhism was providing all that was necessary for mature spiritual development, an aspect of religion which the Catholic church had singularly failed to provide. Nikki

felt that basic cultural differences made it extremely difficult for
Europeans to enter into the kind of celebrations in which we had
recently been involved. She particularly felt that guru devotion was not
consistent with the questioning European mind, or the Western concept
of a mature individual. This brought out a lot of opposing historical
interpretation which was interesting in itself but also because both Jose
and Nikki appeared to come from similar backgrounds—from scientific
Catholic families who had stopped any religious practice and had then
been faced with, and rejected, fascism. Listening, I realized that for them
enlightened agnostic liberalism, like Christian's, was no longer enough
and that any cause they discovered and decided to live by would be
rooted in a very personal commitment.

The other lodge—"The Sherpa"—which overlooks the flight
embarkation shed has a more friendly landlord than our taciturn lady and
a greater mixture of guests. Among them is Rosemarie, the elegant
French ex-model who was filming Lama Zopa's arrival at Lawudo. She is
a recent convert of his and she is very ready to tell us how many gifts he
has lavished on her, also to tell us at great length about the pounding of
her heart when she first met him and all the synchronistic happenings
which are binding her closer and closer to him. Alison's reaction to the
repeated telling of this story was to remark "how skilful" Lama Zopa
was, but to advise Rosemarie not to speak so much about his favours to
her because this would make other people jealous. "She is at the
honeymoon stage," Alison added to me. I can well understand that it
might make Maria jealous as she has failed even to make an
appointment with him and has apparently been denied initiation. Alison
saw this as Lama Zopa's deep understanding of her need to be tested. I
wondered if things might have gone more smoothly for her if instead of
unremitting *puja* sessions she had been taking videos of his activities
which could be used for promotion purposes. How cynical I am getting
about all this!

The other guests at The Sherpa are a laid-back American from
Oregon who knows the mountains well, accompanied by a Sherpa friend
who is returning to the States with him; also the young anthropology
student from Aberdeen whom we met at Apple Pie Lodge on our way
up. He is writing his thesis on "Ideas of pollution and purity in Sherpa

rituals." He did not seem to have been to many rituals or to have done much travelling at all. I think he was just enjoying the different lifestyle, making one or two sorties to put on his itinerary and reading what he could find. Perhaps I am being rather unkind, because he is a pleasant fellow and probably always gives the impression that he is not overexerting himself. There is also a young Swiss couple who regret having not flown out when they originally booked because of the lovely weather; they have now been waiting here for a flight for five days already.

All of us have little to do during this waiting time so that the atmosphere is restless, and silence and solitude not easy to maintain. However, I am lucky to have a single room to which I frequently retire. As I lie on my bed my thoughts move backwards and forwards between my past and the present: the childhood that I experienced as so structured and so safe that no other way of being seemed possible at that time; the fluid and uncertain situation we are in at the moment, and what the step after this will be for me—continuing loneliness of widowhood, balanced by the joy of family closeness and humour, and probably the continuing demands for support from friends and clients. Pondering on the influences and relationships within this future possible life, I realize that the inner attentiveness I have been privileged to have the time at Lawudo to develop, and the solitary silence held by my friends there and by the encircling mountains has allowed me to weave a new kind of inner freedom, which the constant pressures of my normal life would not have permitted.

In The Himalaya the Buddhists meditate; I meditate and write. Down in The Sherpa they play cards with an old pack and read dog-eared old paperback detective stories left by other stranded trekkers. All this is good for the proprietor, as to relieve the tension and the boring nature of his food, endless cups of tea are ordered, and he even has some coffee powder. So in his bar the social life goes on while everyone stares out of the windows at the rain, worries how close to their next appointments the time is getting and longs to get out. Here in the evenings we are joined by some locals, including the young Nepali men who run the Royal Nepal Airlines. Then stiffer drinks are ordered, the fire is stoked up and gambling goes on till late. Up in our lodge, though the surroundings are brighter the atmosphere is unfriendly and the food very slow to arrive, but we have to eat here once a day or the charge for our rooms goes up. The Sherpa is the centre of the stranded trekker's life and to The Sherpa all repair at seven every morning to await the reports coming through from Kathmandu to the little control tower on the edge of the airstrip.

Yesterday, when we were all due to fly out, depression was widespread, particularly among those who had not realized that booking a flight did not mean you actually flew. Perhaps the worst hit was Rosemarie, who also had not realized that there was no communication whatsoever with the outside world. It was her mother's birthday and the poor lady had no idea where her daughter was. The tearful Rosemarie pouted and pleaded with the RNA (Royal Nepal Airlines) boys, and everyone rallied round and was sympathetic but it appeared that nothing could be done. Her plight and the waiting increased my feeling of need to communicate with my family as well. I have not been in touch with them for over six weeks. This seemed to inhibit my ability to write in my journal, so I resorted to half a paperback of a John le Carré story which I found on a windowsill at The Sherpa among back copies of the *Kathmandu Times* and a magazine published in English in Singapore which was two years old. During the day I regained my equilibrium by recognizing how this powerlessness is an aspect of life which I ought to be coming to terms with and which, in our civilization, we have grown quite unaccustomed to. We are so used to being able to pick up a telephone when we want to communicate with someone, so as to express our concern or affection. I thought of the thousands of separated families in the days of the Raj. A voyage of five or six weeks between them and any news of each other: news of their children sent back to England to school, news of recovery from illness or news of a birth or death perhaps more than two months before. What seems such an anachronism here is the little plane—such a modern toy—yet useless against the cloud and rain. Then there are only a few hours in twenty-four when the little toy-like tower is in radio communication with Kathmandu. To the locals this is an accepted part of the technology; to us its limitations seem to increase the sense of isolation.

Yesterday two German boys arrived at The Himalaya, soaking, frozen and hungry, having taken four days walking across two steep valleys from Jiri. At 6:30 this morning they were already having breakfast and planning to walk on to Namche. The seven-o'clock gathering of civil aviation staff, RNA officials and anxious travellers is an interesting time of anticipation as well as tension. This morning the cloud cover was so heavy that few people even bothered to get up. Alison and the two Spaniards were still asleep in the dormitory and Christian and Nikki in their room. Leaving my stuff ready to pack quickly if the weather turned better, I went down the steep path and slippery uneven stone steps covered in cowdung to the Sherpa Lodge. There only Reuben the American was about. We discussed yesterday's reactions of the waiting trekkers to our frustrating experiences. The landlord kept the stove warm and our spirits up with cups of coffee. The RNA boys and some Sherpa porters came in. The cloud remained. Card games began; other sleepy and depressed characters with flights to catch in Kathmandu, deadlines and contacts to meet in other places, began to arrive from houses and lodges in the village, order food or drink and fall silent. There was less rebellion than yesterday, more humour and laughter. People already shared a fund of jokes which had been going round. The silences were less ominous. The RNA second man, isolated in Lukla himself from his wife and two small children in Kathmandu, spoke good English. We had an interesting conversation about American foreign policy. He asked me about Thatcher and the changes which had occurred in England during my lifetime, also whether I thought change should come gradually, or swiftly as in Russia. I took some time to get used to his intonation when he spoke quickly but soon I could follow how his mind was working. The Nepalese want change so much and as quickly as they can get it.

By about 10:30 the cloud began to lift and as the sun came through it revealed clearly the whole length of the valley up which the plane would fly. But the sun was too late, the runway too waterlogged. The decision had already been taken with the control tower during the short time in the early morning when contact was possible. Another claustrophobic day in Lukla; another day for Westerners to develop that unlikely virtue of patience. Lunch at The Sherpa brought all the assorted characters closer together. The two Spaniards had left, walking back to Lawudo to rejoin their guru, who was also cloud-bound. Perhaps Alison would have gone with them if I had not been around. The rest of us did not regret their departure as it took two people off the waiting list. My RNA friend said he would have got us all on a plane if we had been able to fly today. Someone spilt the tomato sauce on a pack of cards. A few heads looked up; a desultory conversation continued. It was agreed that if it did not rain today we might make it tomorrow. Yesterday the cows and dzo all went berserk in the afternoon, charging up and down the steep paths and across the airstrip. This afternoon a very placid black beast is lying in front of my window and some small boys are playing shuttlecock on the airstrip. I climbed up the rocky hill behind this lodge and sat among the rhododendrons looking down on the life of Lukla in the sunshine.

Immediately below me the painfully thin young Hindu woman who lives in a wooden shed off our approach path was cutting up the small goat whose throat her husband had slit in the same place yesterday. Sitting watching her on the doorstep of the shed was her small boy, also painfully thin, and in a basket beside her a tiny baby that she normally carries on her back. The torn plastic nailed over the one window of her shed flaps in the wind. She is an exceptionally beautiful woman with enormous eyes and delicate hands. Living this side of the airstrip seems to indicate that they are somehow not part of the village. The only other buildings beside the lodges are the house and barns of the farmer who owns the cows and dzo. I guess that the woman's husband works for farmers in the hills in exchange for food. On the village side of the airstrip where the children play, many houses and little shops run down both sides of the uneven stony path which forms the village street. A Hindu *saddhu* arrived yesterday with a red turban, white umbrella and all his possessions in a bag on his back. The children are following him around. Women and men stand in their doorways chatting and others are carrying loads up the street or filling in potholes which have become puddles after the rain yesterday. There is a much wider variety of dress than in the higher regions of the Solu Khumbu. On the steps of the building on the corner of the street nearest to the airstrip, a Sherpa woman sits and breastfeeds her baby. Above her head a battered sign:

"Welcome to Paradise Lodge and Restaurant. Rooms with attached toilet and Bar." Above me to the right, approached by a steep path slippery after the rain, is a small wooden building saying "Medical Centre". The birds call on the mountain behind me and the children shout and laugh on their great wide playground which slopes away into the valley at such a steep gradient that it is hard to believe there is enough flat space for even a small plane to take off or land.

One of the great reliefs for me here is the chance to have a change of conversation from "guru devotion"—for only four of the immediate characters at the centre of the waiting drama are Buddhists. I am afraid my silences from time to time during the endless conversation about Lama Zopa may have shown my boredom more obviously than I would have liked. The wonder is so naive, the conclusions they come to always point to powers beyond the ordinary in quite ordinary words or actions. It is a credulity which leaves me uneasy for the future of these devotees. I long to see some of them growing up. So do the German economist, Christian, and his daughter, with whom I have discussions round our experiences here and at Lawudo. During these days together in enforced proximity I have been aware of many different kinds of silences between people and between words. There have been silences like mine which have been substitutes for words that might give offence; there have been silences we have all left as gaps in conversation when we have not been aware of the correct interpretation of what has just been said or in replying to questions we are ambiguous about, as well as the silences I have remarked as an increasingly depressed response to our situation. This kind of silence began in the early hours yesterday and has even seeped into the drinking and games of cards. As the sun came out this morning there was a silence like an indrawn breath, then as time for contact with Kathmandu passed the silence seemed a kind of acceptance of our powerlessness. It produced a few smiles, a silent recognition that we are an odd lot in an odd situation.

Thursday 14 June

Alison and I have now been here four days, others longer. A revolt is brewing because the decision that the weather is unsuitable or the airstrip too wet is taken so early in the morning. If the deadline could be two hours later most of us could have got away yesterday. Christian seems fairly relaxed that his boss will have already arrived in Kathmandu from Germany, expecting him to be there. Other people are getting more agitated about missed commitments, including some of the local people. In the early afternoon a mixed group of protesters arrived at The Sherpa. There was an Indian trader, stranded for four days, who suggested we make a joint complaint. Then there was a discussion about who we should complain to because it appears there is already friction between the young man who is employed by the aviation authority in Kathmandu to make the decisions with them over the radio-telephone and the RNA staff who are responsible to the airline and its passengers. The RNA boss is an autocratic chap we have named Green Cap after his jaunty headgear, who refuses to take any responsibility. It was decided that the first visit of the protesters' group should be to the aviation ministry man. So we set off for his bungalow on the edge of the airstrip, where we discovered him deep in the study of economics, surrounded by an impressive collection of English books and quite nonplussed at our appearance. Without admitting culpability he agreed that his brief report on the visibility and state of the runway at six in the morning ought to be supplemented by a report on the outlook later. After modest disclaimers and somewhat embarrassed noises, he said he had taken note and would convey our protest to his superiors, but that decisions about aircraft movements were the responsibility of RNA. I think we managed to make it clear we did not hold him responsible personally.

Then, gathering local support and interest on the way, we advanced down the stony village street to the airline office, a room in the front of a small house. There we came up against Green Cap, who we knew from the evening gatherings at The Sherpa as a self-opinionated Nepali, given to drinking and then talking too much. He tried to browbeat us and I could see we would have to allow him plenty of room to save face—not so easy with our lot, or in view of the local Sherpa support. After some histrionics (he had heard on the village grapevine of our impending arrival and changed into his best suit) he agreed that a representative of the passengers should be present the following morning in the control tower when he had his decisive conversation with Kathmandu airport. In the pouring rain we trooped back to our lodgings feeling that though we could have no influence on the weather, we had made our protest clear to the two representatives of the bureaucracies responsible for the airstrip. That evening Green Cap, wearing his ordinary clothes, reappeared at Sherpa Lodge and did more than his usual amount of drinking. It was apparent that one of the sensitive areas we had tapped into was that between the "officials" on contract up here from Kathmandu—who are always Nepali and probably Hindu—and the local people, as well as the Sherpa and Tibetan traders and businessmen who use the planes and were supporting us—and are probably Buddhist. You cannot move far in Nepal without encountering these religious and ethnic divisions as well as the antagonism between the ordinary people and the bureaucrats.

At six the next morning I saw Christian—who had been designated our representative—go alone to the control tower. After a short wait he returned with the news. Four planes would come into Lukla during the morning to get everyone who had been waiting back to Kathmandu! Though in the event only two came, this was a triumph. Green Cap was soon at the embarkation building claiming that it was all his doing. The rest of us rushed to pack up and get some breakfast, for though visibility was no better than this time yesterday, it was clear that everyone was anxious to get this awkward bunch of people out of Lukla. At about seven we could hear a plane circling round in the clouds above us, then through a small break the pilot swooped down onto the soggy airstrip. The "Injies" were lined up to go off first—obvious favouritism—plus Reuben's Sherpa friend and one or two of our fellow demonstrators. Then another plane swooped over the mountains across the valley and up onto the airstrip to the accompaniment of cheers from The Sherpa, whose landlord had been one of our most ardent backers. There were also shouts and clapping from the village side, delighted at the climbdown of bureaucracy. Almost everyone who had been waiting more than a couple of days was got onto the planes when a helicopter, which had apparently failed to land at Mende to pick up Lama Zopa, also managed to land in a space near the village. The contrast in the amount of activity on the airstrip compared with the last five days was paradoxical. I wondered how often the pat replies—"No flight. Cloud cover. Wet runway"—were habitual when it suited the airline to have its planes in other places. However, all such thoughts were inappropriate for, as our pilot put the nose of his little plane towards the cloud-filled valley below us, I wondered how he could possibly make it down the steep wet airstrip. These pilots are really skilled at handling their small planes with virtually no instrumentation. We all cheered as he pulled on the joystick and turned the rising plane to avoid the mountains ahead. As the grey fog closed behind us there was no time to turn round and wave farewell to the Solu Khumbu. We soon emerged into bright sunlight and passing over the mountains and increasingly green and cultivated landscape felt the heat of the plains rising towards us even before we had touched down at Kathmandu.

Epilogue

It has taken me much longer than I hoped to transcribe the notes I made day by day in Nepal. On my return the diverse occupations of my usual life closed around me, forcing me to take slowly the process of assessing my experience. Meanwhile the wheel of karma has also been turning for my Lawudo friends.

At the end of the year that I was there Lama Zopa Rinpoche took his family—his mother Amala, his sister Anila and his brother Sangay—to Dharmsala to hear the teachings of His Holiness the Dalai Lama. By this time the old lady had grown increasingly weak. It gave her great pleasure that the day they left on their return journey through Veranasi, the Dalai Lama was with her. For it was in that city, holy to both Buddhists and Hindus, that she died and was cremated on the banks of the Ganges. I mourned for Anila when I heard this news. For some time she felt overwhelmed and as if she had taken on her mother's infirmities. Now, over a year later, I have happier reports of her from Lawudo, where she and Norbu remain the central figures. Thubten Drolkar has moved to Kopan to be a nun, so Anila has a new helper. The blind Cherok Lama was still alive but "showing a very impermanent aspect," as Merry reported. She and her husband had visited and rebuilt the lower cells, which were my first habitation and from which I was flooded out.

So much of my negativity while I was there to this experience of Tibetan Buddhism has fallen away and in many ways I would like to alter some of my journal to reflect my increased understanding, but I have left it as I wrote it in

*order to remain faithful to how it was then. Perhaps my expectations were
unrealistic. I longed to find the common ground, the shared experience, but
somehow we never met at the spiritual level, only at the practical. In my
previous encounters with other faiths this common ground had always been
silent meditation together. At Lawudo we never shared in this way until the
celebration of Nyung Na. When I encountered aspects of Buddhism which I
did not understand I sometimes regretted having no books or experienced guide
to turn to. This was the loneliest part of my journey. It taught me eventually
the art of letting-go of intellectual questions. It also taught me how subtly my
mind continued to avoid learning the art of letting-go of myself and allowing
things to happen, as Eckhart teaches.*

*Despite the sense of privilege, as well as thankfulness, with which I
returned, I realize that the common experience of the greatest value is our
shared humanity and that all spiritual paths which lead us beyond ourselves
also affirm the divine within each one of us. This becomes real for me over and
over again in everyday life. It was to help to leave words behind and anchor
myself in silence and day-to-day experiences, that I had taken only two books.
In spite of often regretting this when I was alone in my cell, as soon as I was
outside, the sight of the snow sparkling in the sun on the high peaks, the
fragile flowers and the bright birds all became more potent guides and gurus
than any supportive or explanatory words could have been. In them I took
refuge while reporting in my journal these ordinary responses of a doubting
and struggling Christian, increasingly aware of how difficult it was to move
beyond the cultural and religious concepts which form the limitations of a
lifetime. It is tempting, more than a year later, to try to modify or explain these
limitations, but this would distort the immediacy of what I wrote and would
only be an attempt to rescue myself from myself.*

*Nevertheless I am convinced that no religions in our modern world can
remain sealed containers of tradition and knowledge as they were in the past. I
wanted to live as closely as possible to this fascinating tradition which had so
impressed people like Thomas Merton, but I had to be content to do this simply
at the human level. The agents for change in all the great religions have been*

individual people and the lives they have lived. "In the depth of every religion there is a point at which the religion itself loses its importance, and that to which it points breaks through its particularity, elevating it to spiritual freedom ..." [1]

My ordinary life, made possible, exciting and humorous by the kindness I met at Lawudo, helped me to resolve so many of the contradictions which had no resolution at the conceptual level and to approach a position of such freedom. For there I met compassion lived out in simple terms, and the way I responded came from the ground of my own belief. We could look into one another's eyes with trust and love. I am not sure whether I kept an open mind but I do know I kept an open heart.

---

[1] Paul Tillich, *Christianity and the Encounter of World Religions,* p97

Glossary

A few Tibetan or Nepali words that became second nature during my time at Lawudo:

bhakti—devotion

bodhicitta—openmindedness

bodhisattva—person who has attained enlightenment but chooses to remain in this life to help others (p61, 96)

B'on—the old animistic religion of the Himalayan region (p58)

chang—home-made beer

chuva—a garment (p29)

dharma—in Buddhism, universal truth; doctrine

dorje—small ceremonial sceptre representing the male principle (p152)

dzo—hybrid of cow and yak

gompa—temple

karma—a fundamental concept in Hindu and Buddhist thought, that the sum of one's actions in this life determines one's fate in the next; destiny

kata—symbolic white scarf given as an offering

lingam—phallus: Buddhism in Nepal incorporates the symbol of the Hindu god Shiva

malla—a circle of wooden beads; a rosary

mani—stone with carved prayers

mo—used like dice, for predicting

momo—dumpling with vegetable filling

mudra—hand movement, a form of prayer

naljorpa—an early lama lineage (p55)

namaste—a greeting (p113)

puja—prayer

rakshi—Sherpa spirits, like rum

rinpoche—a reincarnated teacher

saddhu—Hindu holy man

sangha—fellowship, community

stupa—a stepped tomb, shrine, often with a dome

thangka—a holy picture, ikon

torma—clay figure given as an offering

tsampa—much-processed barley (p75)

t'ai chi—Chinese meditation of movement